BLACK LIKE IT IS/WAS

Erskine Caldwell's Treatment

of Racial Themes

by

WILLIAM A. SUTTON

The Scarecrow Press, Inc.

Metuchen, N. J.   1974

Library of Congress Cataloging in Publication Data

Sutton, William Alfred, 1915–
   Black like it is/was.

   Bibliography: p.
   1. Caldwell, Erskine, 1903–   —Political and
social views. I. Title.
PS3505.A322Z88   813'.5'2   74-5389
ISBN 0-8108-0723-8

Poem, "Did You Ever?", p. xvii, by Theresa Greenwood; reprinted by permission of the author from One Nation Indivisi-
ble, report of Muncie (Indiana) Human Rights Commission,
1972.

this book

is dedicated to

all the black people
who have added to my life

and to the work of Erskine Caldwell,
which has done the same

FOREWORD*

by Theresa Greenwood

Erskine Caldwell's vivid narratives of how blacks were treated and mistreated in the old order of the South can still arouse extreme anger and bitterness. It can make a conscience-stricken white cringe when he vicariously relives those days of black degradation; and it can puncture the irreparable wounds of blacks who feel they will never fully recover from the three hundred-year-old malaise. Caldwell's account of how blacks were used by whites for everything from personal libidinal gratification to collective capitalistic gain has left a definitive record for history. The malevolent acts that Caldwell depicts reveal the depths to which one race stooped to make themselves superior. For, during and after slavery, whites took advantage of a still-primitive people and made it a national mission to keep them ignorant and enslaved.

And many blacks believe this mission is still in effect. The dogs have not been called off and millions of black Americans are still locked in symbolic, economic and psychological chains. The pursuit of justice, liberty and economic equality is not yet a reality for all men, especially blacks. Although a fleeting few have been able to approach these goals, the majority of blacks still remain in the mire of yesterday's crippling inequities.

Following his arrival in the new world, the black man quickly became a castigated tool: useful when he was needed and superfluous property to be sold and traded like cattle when he had served out his purpose. He was torn from his family with no regard for his ties to kin and off-spring and friends. He was like an ox, auctioned off for stud service, purchased for his wide, strong back and sinewy muscles or kept as a Paphian slave for the master's lecherous bent.

The black man had been historically an asset during the struggling days of this nation, but as soon as technology could be substituted for brawn he was no longer needed or even tolerated. He became a handy whipping boy and was thrown about by the whims of those he came in contact with. Also, to many whites, he was just that illiterate darkie who, according to some, was created by God to be a slave. And since he was born with less brain mass he could never be trusted to think clearly, constructively and make mainline decisions. He never grew up and achieved manhood; he was forever doomed to be a BOY! He was created to serve and entertain his captors, for they knew what was best for him. And he would be content just as long as he had a piece of land to tend, a tankard of wine, lilting music and maddening rhythm.

Since most primitive peoples have always worshipped the sun for one reason or another, these early blacks believed that anything that was white or light must have come from god. These loyal slaves soon associated this belief with their captors. Since they were white, indeed they must have been earthly manifestations of powers and gods to be feared, worshipped and served, and even imitated. This attitude existed down through the centuries in the relationships between blacks and whites. Black people feared the white man, thus making scare tactics effective with the gullible and fearful slaves.

Black people even sought to become "white." They attempted to lighten their skins, unkink their hair and emulate other characteristics. The blacks had become so awed with whiteness that at one time blacks even rejected their own people who had darker skins and black children preferred to play with white dolls (a trend which has now reversed itself). Blacks worshipped whiteness until blackness became a source of negative reinforcement they all attempted to avoid. They had learned through conditioning and reconditioning that white was right and black was bad. But during the black renaissance, blacks began to realize that they must accept themselves and be proud of what they were. This philosophy ushered in the natural lifestyle which has had far-reaching ramifications in setting trends for hairstyles, make-up and dietary habits around the world. It was not until the last few years that blacks have purposedly confronted their own blackness and systematically organized their defense against their subjugation.

Blacks who had suffered the humiliation of capture and slavery were destined to suffer as well the personal impudence and irrationality of their captors, who were intent on making them less than human. The generalizing effects of this attitude have affected the way white people perceive the black man even today. For example, blacks may be those intruders who moved into the neighborhood and became a cultural and psychological threat to those living there. They may be those unfortunate people living on the other side of the tracks who are remembered twice a year with bulging baskets and holiday "love."

They may be those kinky-head militants, dressed in long dazzling dashikis, whose very nature is seething with hate and violence and who may creep into the suburbs one quiet night and take over. Or, as many believe, they are those lazy, good-for-nothings who prefer to live in filth, who do not really want to work and who beg and stay on welfare. And if you let them live in a nice place, they will surely tear it up and destroy all that is good, decent and beautiful. As a result of these attitudes, perpetuated from one generation to another, the Sixties were marked with excessive flight by whites from the blacks. For example, some areas in larger cities changed from as little as 3 percent to 90 percent black within the last five years.

But as whites sought refuge in the suburbs, blacks came to comprise the largest voting block in the cities. As a result many dramatic political changes took place and now many whites are beginning to move back into the cities, although they are so far successfully escaping the threat of racial integration by nesting safely in highrise condominiums which are priced out of the range of the average black family. This type of economic discrimination keeps the schools and neighborhoods free from hordes of encroaching blacks. The latest statistics (see, e.g., Time, September 3, 1973, pages 73-75) tell us that the black man still suffers from declining incomes, educational inferiority and social isolation. Even after the Movements of the Fifties and Sixties to overcome their oppressors, black people as a whole have still not advanced. Only a "slim wedge" of Black Americans have benefitted.

Blacks did not, as some would have us believe, choose this way of life. It was thrust upon them. For if a people have a choice between opulence and poverty, between wisdom and ignorance, between power and subjugation, who would choose the least of these?

The beginnings of the black man's plight can be
traced back to the mood and climate created during the
earliest days of slavery. Blacks were then and until recently victims of a system that did not permit them to make
their own choices. They have been dictated to for these
past three hundred years and it has not been until the last
decade that they even had an opportunity to have a say in
the destiny of their own lives. Up until that time their
minds, emotions and bodies were ravished by plunderers of
black flesh and black soul. Even with the widely intended
lessening of tensions and increased opportunities, many
blacks say, "This is still a white man's world and baby
don't you forget it!" Still others say, "Whitey is letting
us gather some of the crumbs off the floor, but he'll never
let us see the cake." These blacks are bitter. They feel
they have nothing to lose by confronting whites head-on with
violence. But this trend has been abandoned by many, for
it was soon evident that the old proverb was true: violence
only begets violence.

Other blacks believe the conscience (and complacency)
of whites has been sufficiently pricked and that the former
oppressors are now seeking to make retribution for the long-
standing injustices of the past. They believe we are in the
greatest era of racial cooperation and advancement. They
have taken a look at the limited progress made in the sports
arena and in the political world and have attempted to par-
allel it with the progress of all blacks. While it is true
that there have been several isolated cases of blacks who
have "made it," the fact remains that the masses of blacks
are still prisoners in political and social ghettos.

In order to insure that the days reminiscent of Caldwell's books would never become ingrained again in the
American psyche, blacks attempted systematically to reject,
revolt against, and re-fashion their plight. Numerous black
organizations were revived and others formed to counteract
white conservative organizations and to serve as a basis for
binding blacks together for unity of purpose and direction.
Yet history shows us that the impact of these efforts was
not totally effective. Even so, this genesis of black action
brought about fear among certain whites and served to
polarize them.

Whites came to feel threatened by the explosive tinder

of black dress, language, attitudes and organizations. This
created the climate for some of the extreme southern political figures to emerge during this time. They had a special appeal to the poor whites of the South and North.
These vociferous wizards built "white castles" in the dreams
of their followers and promised that once again WHITE
would reign supreme. It was a salvation to many whites
who had literally taken a back seat to those blacks who,
they felt, were gaining politically and economically. Some
whites made it clear to blacks who "made it" that they must
remember they were just being extended the privileges--it
was not their right; after all, they had once been slaves.

By the time of the Sixties, blacks were literally
getting it together in many areas. They had only one mission: to break the chains that bound them and their children
and continued to threaten their future generations. The cost,
they reasoned, might be high; but many felt that sacrifice
was in order, to assure that their children's children would
sleep in delicious comfort. Blacks began to enter the universities in increasing numbers; they were "tolerated" in
white neighborhoods. And there were increased efforts from
whites to impress upon those blacks who had "made it" that
they were different. These attitudes offended the masses
of blacks and caused sustained breaks that continued to
grow. Now, as a result, blacks live in worlds separate
from each other, some by choice, some by circumstance,
some by coercion. In these days of supposedly the most
advanced technological and scientific achievement in the recorded history of mankind, men and women have a long way
to go to equal that achievement in their relationships with
one another as human beings.

It may be that in a few short years the bulk of blacks will
be in a much worse political and social position than they
were twenty years ago. There may again be mass segregation, closed political opportunities and increased poverty.
But there will be one major difference: the psychological
impact will not be as critical, because the blacks will have
emotionally accepted the fact that the white world and the
black world really cannot blend and become one. Blacks
will be content to live in the squalid ghettos and send their
children to inferior schools.

They will laugh at and generate the same stereotyped

"nigger humor" which they fought so hard against during the Fifties and Sixties. (The emergence of this trend is now evident in the television programs which still cast the black man as a lazy, stupid, jiving clown. One has yet to see a "normal, average, intact" black family depicted on television!) It may be that blacks themselves will accept the pickaninny peering from behind the watermelon, the wide, loyal, toothy grin of Aunt Jemima, and be proud and call it all: "our heritage." And black men will walk with pride in the street with hair styles reminiscent of female slaves and don the bizarre designs created just for black folks and shout, "Can you dig it, man?"

All the time the blacks who have "made it" will become refugees and sojourners among their own race, fearful of making contact with their unstable, vacillating roots. They will truly be marginal men. They will be too white to be black and too black to be white. In sum, it seems most blacks are destined to remain in their ghettos and black like it is, will be black like it was.

The black man was destined in time to reject his oppressors and to fight back physically, economically, politically, educationally and psychologically. He counteracted the forces of his degradation and possible annihilation first with servitude and loyalty, then with reason and moral obligation, and finally by force. From the day Rosa Parks, the black woman credited with challenging the segregated system, took that fateful bus ride in Montgomery, Alabama, the old order of the American caste system by race and color had begun to topple. It reeled and cavorted with the wild gyrations of demonstrations, fire-bombings, and sit-ins--waging war, sometimes violently, against racism.

The blacks had been silent while their children were stolen from them and lynched; and while they ate the garbage of an affluent society. The pressures mounted and then exploded: The Sixties were marked with a tragic crisis of race confrontation that shook not only this nation, but the world as well. Within a few years, religious and political leaders realized that they had remained silent while grave lesions were growing upon the nation. Many whites took the yoke of brotherhood more seriously than ever before and marched alongside blacks in their quest for equality. It soon became fashionable to care for one's black brother or

sister. It seemed to some that the age of Aquarius was
indeed dawning and it would not be long before blacks and
whites would walk off hand-in-hand into the peaceful sunset.

But during those crisis-filled days, contending blocks
of Americans seemed also to suffer even greater schisms.
On the surface, things seemed to be working out, but under-
neath, greater currents of a more serious nature were
swelling. Attention was snatched from the cries of the black
man. It was quickly pointed out that he was not the only
one suffering abuse because of superficial differences. Before too long one minority after another joined the ranks of
the segregated, the forgotten, the lost. The lines got longer
and the longer they got the further away was the solution the
black man was seeking. His plight was now overshadowed
by others whose cries drowned his out.

While it is true that the plight of all oppressed
peoples should be righted, it seemed that the droning claims
of other groups who already enjoyed more freedom and privileges than blacks were now serving to cover up the real
misery of the millions of other Americans who were still
enslaved. As a result the plight of the black man today has
become much like that of the freed slave following the Civil
War. During that time blacks were indulged. Just as today: they became judges, community leaders, mayors, even
governors. The blacks were put into positions of authority
by vengeance-seeking Northerners who sought to punish the
treasonous Southern whites. Although the blacks were not
really in control, they were used by Northern businessmen
as pawns. (So it may be that blacks are again pawns,
existing only at the base of ivory-white towers from whose
heights come the manipulations of invisible strings.) As a
result, blacks were and are still not trusted by Southern
whites. Blacks became an economic and social threat to
the South and clandestine societies and threatful activities
were organized to keep them in their "place. " The organized
debasement of black men, black women, their families,
values, and character--as depicted in Caldwell's work--re-
minds those who choose to listen that there is much hurt to
be undone.

The economic/cultural opportunity of the Sixties was a by-
word for the black man. Social and governmental programs
were often threatened with crippling failures. Communication

breakdowns existed between agencies and government, between black people and white people, and between black
people and black people. As a result a third force began to
rise in the Sixties. It was a mutation due to the circumstance the so-called "conservative black man" had found
himself in. This black man usually had not actively participated in the demonstrative efforts of the more militant.
Although theirs had been spiritual and emotional support of
demonstrations, these blacks often sought gains through education, reason and economic levers.

The schisms grew wider because the blacks were now
separating among themselves by their hairstyles, their dress
and language. There was increased interest, in some circles,
in learning the "mother tongue"; some talk resembling the
days of Marcus Garvey with back-to-Africa slogans and projects. Black Power was an explosive call which had different meanings for different blacks and whites. Polariza-
tion began to take place within the black community itself.
Blacks were no longer "Negroes." They were Afro- or
Black-Americans. Those who were not as vocal as others
were called Uncle Toms. But the more conservative blacks
often felt it was necessary to make the sacrifice of rejection
by their own people in order to make realistic gains in
equality. (As a result of the throes of the Sixties, everybody became a hyphenated American. There are now Black-
Americans, Afro-Americans, Mexican-Americans, Irish-
Americans, and so on. Will there ever come a day, when
we will all be proud just to be Americans?)

This wedge of conservative, striving blacks began to
separate themselves physically, spiritually and economically
from their brothers who did not make it to the "promised
land." This schism, some believe, may have been subtly
created by those who see it more profitable to keep the black
man confused and without single direction and purpose. The
masses of blacks came closest to this goal under leaders
who were prematurely snatched from among them. And now
they clamor about without unity and direction.

This third force of conservative blacks that emerged
has a social and economic future still unpredictable. But
there are a couple of hypotheses we might explore. One is
that the blacks who crossed the "River Jordan" will be ab-
sorbed socially, physically and politically into the main-
stream of America. This powerful, affluent minority wedge
will be (and is) seen as getting too big, too educated, too

powerful--too difficult to keep under control. So: more
and more blacks are being channeled into less viable careers
and efforts increase to steer blacks away from college.

Some blacks who wish to follow their more affluent
brothers and sisters are fighting back. Black parents are
pushing for education and environment that can foster the
best social and intellectual development. They believe that
"a child conceived in the midst of hate, sin and discord,
nurtured on abuse and injustice cannot do much to bless the
world or himself. " They are encouraging their children to
get college educations regardless of trends and so-called
racist counseling efforts. Black parents are revolting
against the "voucher system" and "open education" which
could subtly deny the motivated and perpetuate inferior neighborhood schools. The black man sees education as well as
business as the two most important power tools for escaping
his oppression. Some black parents are also against the
campaigns for reducing the size of families, as they feel
this is one way to qualitatively and quantitively undermine
the power and effect of the black family.

Another hypothesis surrounding the emergence of the
conservative black is that this "wedge" will be used to drive
blacks farther and farther apart, leaving them continually
divided among themselves and never totally achieving as
have other minority racial groups in the history of the U. S.
Black people would then wander again in the wilderness--
and the spiraling cycle will begin all over again.

> Why do we wait for people to explode be-
> fore we stop to listen to what they are
> saying?

Theresa Greenwood, Mrs. Charles H. Greenwood, is the
author of Psalms of a Black Mother (Anderson, Ind. : The
Warner Press, 1970).

CONTENTS

Did You Ever?

Did you ever see
    a lukewarm
    crooked smile
    forced through clenched teeth...
    only to see it snatched up and
    swallowed
    before you passed by?

Did you ever feel
    the hard hose of hate
    coil and
    rip your eternal dreams?

Did you ever hear
    the nasty concerto of
    jeers clanging like cymbals in your soul?

Did you ever touch
    a helpless trembling pale heart
    out of pity out of
    compassion...
    only to be burned with the fires of hate?

If you have ever...
Then you know what it's like
to be
Black.

Theresa Greenwood
1969

But I have not finished what I have to say
about the people in the novel that has been
suppressed, I have an intense sympathy for
these people. I know them and I like them.
I have slept with them in jails, I have eaten
with them in freight cars, I have sung
with them in convict camps. I have helped
the women give birth to the living, I have
helped the men cover up the dead.... I
have said that I know these people, that I
love them.*

---

*From "In Defense of Myself," a broadside published by
Erskine Caldwell in Portland, Maine, on the occasion of
the suppression of his first published book, The Bastard, in
February 1930.

I. ERSKINE CALDWELL AND GEORGIA*

Probably the most important thing about Erskine Caldwell, after the fact that he is a sensitive Southerner--a
Georgian--who grew up in the early part of this century, is
that he is a writer of fiction. Anything that he has written
in his many books about Georgia, and the South, and even
what he says about his life there has to be seen through
the significance of his craft. It is true that his writings
include reportorial work, books of travel. He even worked
for most of a year (from September 1925 to May 1926) on
the Atlantic Journal (concurrently with the lady then known
as Peggy Mitchell). But it has not been possible to find
one identifiable newspaper article about Georgia written by
Erskine.

Additionally, it could be helpful to know just how long
Erskine lived in Georgia. He was born to the Rev. and
Mrs. Ira S. Caldwell, he being the pastor of White Oak
Associate Reformed Presbyterian Church, in the parish
house on what is now R. R. 6, Newnan, Georgia, in Coweta
County, on December 17, 1902. The parish house is situ-
ated on a farm road several miles from the church, which
still stands on another country road. If the reader examines
any of the existing literature on Caldwell, it will be found
that his birthdate is given as 1903. The records which
show that it was really 1902 also indicate that it was while
he was a student at the University of Virginia that he started
to refer to himself as born in 1903. A year after he recognized that the evidence indicated he was born in 1902, he
still referred to himself as being born in 1903. It would be
futile to discuss this fact with Caldwell, who probably would
quite honestly say he had no idea why he preferred 1903.
Similarly, it may be assumed that any other actualities of a

---

*This is a revised version of the author's "Georgia on His
Mind," which originally appeared in the Douglas (Georgia)
Enterprise, January 25, 1973.

fiction writer's life may be arbitrarily changed, in artistic
creations or in the artist's recollection of life as lived.

The records of his father's pastorate show that the
family left the assignment at the White Oak Church, which
has seats for about thirty people, in June 1906. The next
time the Caldwells lived in Georgia was in 1919, in July of
which year the Rev. Caldwell was called to the Associate
Reformed Presbyterian Church in Wrens, where he was
pastor until his death in 1944. Erskine lived in Wrens from
July of 1919 until he went to Erskine College in Due West,
S. C. , in September of 1920. During the summer of 1920
he worked as a stone mason's helper in Calhoun, Georgia,
helping to build a Baptist church which still stands. He
got the job through an aunt; his uncle, Richard Hines, had
a shoestore in Calhoun.

Once he left to go to Erskine College, Wrens was
just the home place Caldwell visited at various times. He
went home for vacations. When he ran away from Erskine
in January of his second year there, he returned to Wrens
for the rest of the spring and summer before he went back
to school in the fall. When he was graduated from what was
then known as Wrens Institute in 1920, he really hoped he
might go to the University of Georgia or some similar school.
But both his parents had attachments to Erskine College; his
father recruited students for it and his mother taught at its
women's annex. Both economic and emotional factors sent
him to this college, which, in his more adjusted moods, he
tolerated.

In September 1923, through the Daughters of the Confederacy of Georgia, he got a "scholarship" to the University
of Virginia, the basis for which was his relationship to those
who had fought for the Confederacy rather than his disen-
chanted and unmotivated, even rebellious, record at Erskine.
At the end of that first year at Charlottesville, he went
home, supposedly for the summer, and told his parents he
wanted to go to the University of Pennsylvania to study economics. They took him as far as they could in the family
Ford, and he spent the summer there on a shoe string.
He returned home at Christmas, just before going back for
another try at the University of Virginia.

When Caldwell rather suddenly married the daughter
of a faculty member at the University of Virginia, he brought
her home to Wrens to meet his parents. So little was known

in advance about this matter that the local paper said the
bride was from Pennsylvania.   During this marriage, which
lasted from 1925 until 1938, Erskine and his wife and
children, of which there came to be three, often visited in
Wrens, especially, it would appear, during their 1925-1926
stay in Atlanta.   Sometimes the visits would be for several
months.   His father even arranged with an Augusta doctor
for Caldwell to use a fishing shack on the Savannah River
as a place to hole up and write.   Erskine's wife, Helen,
and the children might stay in Wrens or go to Charlottesville
on occasion.   As young married people, visiting, they would
be invited to various parties, as at the Country Club on
occasion.   Then, after 1927 and until 1937, Erskine and
Helen lived in Portland and near Augusta, Maine.

Caldwell brought his second wife, Margaret Bourke-
White, to Wrens at Christmas, 1941, to report to a gathering held in his father's church on what they had seen in
Russia.   There were many visits to Georgia.   It would be
arduous to either count or chronicle them, but they were
just visits.   However, in spite of the short time he lived
there, Georgia was much on his mind.

In November 1926, Caldwell published in an obscure
magazine his first work, an article called "The Georgia
Cracker" [reprinted as the first item in the addenda].
Stemming from a writing assignment in a class at the Uni-
versity of Virginia, this portrait is most unflattering.   He
says that during his work as a reporter the "truth about the
Georgia Cracker filtered through to me. "   He refers to
Georgia's "barbarism in education, religion, and justice. "
Probably no one in Georgia read the article, and his fellow
Georgians did not know until Tobacco Road appeared how
critical he was of what he saw.

Poems he wrote while he was at the University of
Virginia (so far unpublished) show a concern for the Georgia
scene.   Most of his early writings began to get published in
"little" magazines as early as 1929.   They often dealt with
the Georgia scene--more often than not--but the Georgia
reader would not have encountered them.   Of two still unpublished works by Caldwell found in a window seat at the
home of Margaret Bourke-White shortly before her death in
1971, one had its setting in Portland and the other in two
towns highly reminiscent of Wrens and one of its neighbors.

Of course, Caldwell's most famous books are Tobacco

Road and <u>God's Little Acre</u>. The setting for <u>Tobacco Road</u>
could just as well have been South Carolina as Georgia, because, aside from the observations he made for himself,
the impact on his mind of the socially-disoriented family,
the Lesters, came especially from the deep interest of his
father in people such as they.   Not only did the Rev. Caldwell constantly help the poor and the black in the area of
Wrens, but also he made a study of 250 such families in
Georgia and South Carolina and published a five-article
series on his findings.   <u>Tobacco Road</u> is an artistic rendering of observations that Erskine shared with his father.

Though Erskine has evidently, from the beginning,
shown little tendency to participate in conventional religion,
he was keenly aware of his father's activities and interests.
Much of his work concerns itself with religion.   Certainly
<u>God's Little Acre</u> is, more than anything else, a commentary
on the gap between theory and practice in human religion,
though Caldwell would be reluctant to discuss such an idea.
He customarily says that <u>God's Little Acre</u> is a story about
a man's problems in keeping his family together.   He evidently decided early in his career to avoid all serious discussion of the way his work comments on society.   His work
is filled with social comment, but the reader has to find it
without any help from Caldwell.

As even an Ohioan can find out how totally Georgian
is the seemingly-odd name of Ty Ty given to the main
character of <u>God's Little Acre</u>, it can be expected that many
Georgians who have read Caldwell's works will find that one
of two things, and possibly both, are constantly at work in
his mind as he creates his fiction.   Probably an expert
would have a hard time deciding which Southern factors in
his writing result peculiarly from his life in Georgia--as
opposed to Virginia, Tennessee, North Carolina, South
Carolina, or Florida, all states where he lived, or to others
that he visited and keenly observed.   Perhaps some scenes
and incidents actually come from somewhere else and are
simply placed in a Georgia setting.   The reader is invited
to explore the many books Caldwell wrote that deal with
Georgia, and the many more stories, and see what findings
result, being assured that Georgia was the most important
single location in the geography of Erskine Caldwell's
imagination.

One of the greater literary privileges of this writer's

life has been its enlargement through the writings of Erskine Caldwell, which first came to the writer's attention about thirty-five years ago. In 1968, a correspondence with Caldwell began and at the end of 1969, he agreed to allow the writer to prepare a biography with his approval. Visits to the Caldwell home in Florida, some hours of interviewing, and much correspondence have led to the threshold of some major realizations concerning this uniquely powerful and valuable literary talent. One finds in writing a biography, in gathering the facts about a human life--especially one as complicated and vital as that of Erskine Caldwell--that the process is endless. An especial pleasure has been to try to capture the relationship of a writer to his native state, where he seldom lived but never forgot and to which his creative consciousness was constantly returning. In spite of the fact that his life and work show him to be a courageous man with intense compassion for injury and a passion for justice as he sees it, Erskine Caldwell is very austere as well. He tells things as he sees them. Some people have thought he ought to have seen things differently. And others have thought he ought not tell what he saw.

It was a piece of bad luck that the people who would best understand what he thought was important could not read--or, if they could read, they would never have had enough money to buy a book. And it was just that unsatisfactory aspect of life, especially of black life, that motivated him to write, though it is doubtful he would admit it. An extension of his social criticism was that literate Georgians took it personally. He used the landscape of Georgia often to display imaginatively the amount of improvement humanity still has to make. But he knew as well as anyone else, perhaps better than some, that Georgia, and the South in general, is no more guilty of human frailty than any other place. In a conversation in December 1971, just after he had returned from a trip around the world, he spoke in the most shocked terms of the poverty and depravity of life in Calcutta. It was a lot worse than Tobacco Road.

It is well-known that some Georgians honor the work of Erskine Caldwell. Not only does he have at least three devoted friends in Atlanta, one of whom has known him since Journal days, but also he was given, in 1969, a scroll in honor of his forty years of leadership in the creative arts. When it was a matter of controversy as to whether the

dramatization of Tobacco Road should appear in Atlanta and
Augusta, there were those who sprang immediately to its
defense.   He has been formally introduced and honored at a
session of the Georgia House of Representatives.

But there have been those who disliked his work in-
tensely (and hence him, though they did not know him personally).   Attempts have been made through Georgia state
agencies to ban his works.   Many editorials decrying his
work have appeared in newspapers across the state.   Caldwell's favorite, declaring that he was "an earthworm," was
displayed under the glass top of his desk for many years.
Perhaps he would have liked to be immensely popular in
Georgia, but he was never hail-fellow-well-met in his personal relationships, nor does such a personality emerge in
any way from his writings.   He has generally understood an
active negative reaction to be a sign that his message was
getting attention.

Caldwell has enjoyed considerable economic success.
Approximately eighty million copies of his books have been
sold around the world in fifty languages.   This writer found
an unauthorized Spanish edition in 1972; accurate figures, it
would seem, can never be obtained, although Erskine has
remarkably detailed records.   Through one circumstance and
another, he has become at least very comfortable financially.
(He seems like a typical farmer of any state, in that he will
never admit he has a surplus of money.   One friend said he
would discuss any topic but money.)   He wrote Tobacco
Road, but what catapulted him to fame and fortune was its
dramatization by another writer, Jack Kirkland, whose only
claim to fame is that he adapted Tobacco Road.   In discussing his economic success, the occasion arises to settle
a noxious contention relating to Caldwell's life.   Some people
who did not like his criticisms of the American social structure have called him a Communist.   This accusation has
benefitted by the popularity of his books in Russia (where
books critical of our country often enjoy success), by the
fact that he and Margaret Bourke-White chanced to be in
Russia when Germany attacked in June 1941, and by his obvious belief in liberal causes.   But, as he told a group of
left-wing film writers, "I am not a Communist and never
have been."   The slightest acquaintance with either his personality or his life-style would yield convincing corrobora-
tion of that statement.   Finally, as has been made clear
many times over the years, including quite recently, a

writer as outspoken and individualistic as Erskine, in which
respect he is Georgian to the core, would not last five
minutes under either a Fascist or a Communist regime.

II.   THE WRITER'S PROTEST

Quite late in his career (1968), Caldwell told a lecture audience that his aim had always been "to have movement and freedom and to seek experience in the world." But such statements are just his way of disarming reactions to his protests against what a French critic called "Caldwell's miserable and crazy universe." A friend of forty years wrote in 1965, "Man's inhumanity to man has always been his theme." One evening in 1967, a black friend taped a conversation with Caldwell. He asked him how he became a writer of protest against "brutality, stupidity and so forth." Caldwell replied that he had seen "many inhuman acts" inflicted upon both whites and blacks in Georgia. What he saw was not conducive to the idea of brotherhood among people. He reminded his friend, Ray McIver, of mistreatment of both people and animals which they had both seen, and said, "Now don't get me started on these things because I have too much of a vivid memory of the cruelty I've seen inflicted upon people."

Yet the impact of the subject, once broached, was so strong that when McIver started on another question, Caldwell asked why he wanted to get off the matter of cruelty to people and animals. McIver said he had eighteen other questions he wanted to ask. Caldwell returned, "I know, but when you see mules beaten to death ... and you see humans inflicted almost with death and left almost in the same position a mule would be if he were beaten down --..." Caldwell continued a few minutes later, "I have seen the infliction of cruelty on people on the chain gang both white and Negro, so don't get me started on that or else cut me off completely and I won't say another word about it." McIver assured him he was "just trying to be fair to the rest of my questions." Caldwell reiterated that he was answering the question, why he wrote as he did, by referring to the brutality he had witnessed. "I was not an evangelist or anything, but how can a human being live

without protesting...?'' He continued to make reference to
brutal actions he had known, saying that even when some
of these events were in the past, they left a scar. "Well,
slavery did exist, didn't it? And the scar still lives, all
right. So we should recognize, we shouldn't try to cover
up and say, well, it's in the past ... but I'm a sensitive
person, and I don't like this inhumanity against persons. "

The reactions and convictions which lay behind that
statement of Caldwell may be related to two other known
factors. His personality was one of sensitivity and independence. He recalled his mother's telling him that as a
small child he often disrupted his father's sermons because
he would wriggle off the pew and crawl around under the
other pews. Later, members of the church in Charlotte
(N. C.) were moved to wonder out loud why the minister's
son could not wear shoes to church. Still later, Erskine's
parents, though they both worked devotedly in the church,
did not insist that he attend services. Along with this
sense of independence of action he had a quality of compassion for other creatures. He is remembered as devoted
to animals, and had a dog and a cat as a child (and through
most of his adult life). One of his aunts recalled seeing
him sitting on the steps of his house, holding a dead bird
or chicken he had found, with tears running down his cheeks.

Caldwell has always resisted the idea that sooner
or later occurs to any careful student of his life--that he
was carrying on the ministry of his father. He has far too
strong a sense of his own independence of character and
art to see himself in that role. Yet his father, the Reverend Ira S. Caldwell, spent the years from 1901 to 1944 in
the service of the Associate Reformed Presbyterian Church,
a small, strictly-disciplined sect which had and still has
roughly 20, 000 members in the southeastern part of the
United States. Though he served that church devoutly, he
was known throughout the sect as a radical; among other
things, he spent a good deal of his time and concern on
poor whites and blacks who were not members of his church.
He seems to have shared with his son a sense that all are
equal before God, regardless of superficial differentiations.

Aside from the broadening influence that travel and
residence with his parents in Georgia, Virginia, North
Carolina, South Carolina, Tennessee, and Florida had on
Erskine Caldwell, he took something more vital from his

father particularly. In <u>Deep South</u>, Caldwell records that
he thought his father went into the ministry because of a
commitment to his mother. He suggests that he stayed
in it in spite of a personal deviation from the beliefs called
for by the creed under which he served. The ministry
gave him an opportunity to render service to people, particularly the unfortunate he saw everywhere about him--the
people he pointed out to his son as "toads in post holes."

When a reporter heard Erskine Caldwell give a lecture on writing at the New School in New York in 1939, he
noted a statement that the irritants of life lead to writing.
Erskine recalled that his father was always talking about
the desecration of nations and people. Not content with the
outlet given him by the pulpit, the senior Caldwell conducted
for years a column in first one and then another Augusta
(Georgia) newspaper: his utterances there fully justify the
statement in his obituary, that he gave himself to the awaken-
ing of public conscience. Day by day, as he wrote, he pro-
tested against the way in which the life around him was being
lived, apparently undaunted at the lack of identifiable change.
He openly advocated, time after time, the elimination of injustice and inequality, devoting column after column to examples. He wrote that the Civil War was unnecessary and
regrettable. He expressed his conclusion that the vultures
of life devoured the hope of the poor. As he spent his time,
energy, money, and words on the poor, I. S. Caldwell wrote,
"The world needs a new highway, broad enough to allow the
entire human race to reach a new level." He also wrote,
"The most important problem before the country is to lift
the masses to the level of hope and possible efficiency."
It can not be a surprise that the son of this man wrote, in
<u>Around About America</u> in 1963--nearly twenty years after
his father's death and nearly thirty after he had begun to
express his own rebellion against the conditions he saw
about him--that he thought one could not be a loyal American
if he did not protest against racial discrimination.

Certainly the impulses which led Erskine Caldwell
to build protest into his writing have not become less insistent. Just a month after he returned from a trip around
the world, in December 1971, he said his most vivid impression of the trip was of Calcutta, where "one million people
live on the street." He saw women with babies in arms
soliciting customers for the use of their bodies. He reported masturbation and copulation occurring openly on the

sidewalk. People frequently used the gutters to relieve
their bodies of waste, he noted. Children were observed
foraging for food particles among the garbage and waste
in the slime of the gutters. Sacred cows, untouchable, as
Mrs. Caldwell found when she moved to pet one, everywhere
left their droppings, which women were seen to take into
their hands and make into cakes, which were then sold for
fuel. After reciting those memories in a conversation, he
remarked, "A place like that makes you wonder whether human existence is justified."

He wrote, in an article published in the Saturday Review in 1958, that the way for civilization to justify itself
would be to create a situation in which there was general
respect for the spirit of humans, liberating people instead
of rendering them helpless. And he concluded an article on
censorship for Esquire with what, for him, was the focal
passage in God's Little Acre. He referred to Ty Ty Walden's
saying that people go by the impulses they feel within them,
not by what society, specifically referred to in Ty Ty's
speech as the church, tells them. "When you sit down by
yourself and feel what's in you, that's the real way to live."
And Caldwell says that free spirit should prevail, too, in
the way one writes; he records interestingly the reactions
to existence one has, without fear or favor, in, for example,
the words of the oath the sheriff forgets in Trouble in July.

In that book, as will later be discussed, Caldwell
gives the anatomy of a lynching. The focus of the book on
the mistreatment of blacks is unmistakable. But Caldwell
does not necessarily tell his readers that he is protesting.
In his autobiography, Call It Experience, he blandly says
that the book describes small town politics and its effect
on the lives and character of people of the community. In
another place he came closer to the mark, indicating that
he wanted to illuminate an element of decay in society in
the hope that it would be eliminated. There is no doubt
that Caldwell wished to call the enormity of white racism
and black misery to the attention of society, believing that
when readers knew the truth their protest would join his
own.

III. THE MANIPULATION OF BLACKS

Uncle Jeff, an aging black farmhand in A House in the Uplands (1946), remarks ruefully that perhaps his people should never have come into existence, in view of the way all of their life is fraught with difficulty. That is no way to look at it, a white farmer blandly remarks: without the blacks, the whites would have to do more and harder work. The old black submissively agrees. In his earliest writings, Caldwell was aware of "work-hardened Negroes" (e. g. , in The Bastard, 1929) and black workers who sweat from dawn to dusk without a break for water ("Hours Before Eternity, " ca. 1930). A picture in You Have Seen Their Faces (1937) of a pith-helmeted white overseer in Louisiana is accompanied by the observation that blacks will work twice as hard as whites, like dogs who will obey when beaten.

Caldwell had pointed out in Some American People (1935) that Alabama made a special point of having plenty of blacks to work the fertile cotton lands. Thirty years later he would use In Search of Bisco to aver that the fertile land of the south is pleasant for the whites, but the toil of the blacks has been unrewarded. In The Earnshaw Neighborhood (1971), Frank Earnshaw muses over the fact that he had noticed how poorly paid and housed the black peanut workers were. His grandfather had predicted that the blacks would prove to be cheaper and more reliable than the prospective machinery would be. The replacement of less-capable whites by able-bodied blacks is exemplified repetitively in Caldwell's writings. In You Have Seen Their Faces (1937) mention is made of the routine replacement of the washed-out white sharecropper with a strong, young black. In a discussion of statements about intense sweating (and accompanying odor) on the part of the blacks, as alleged by whites, it is allowed in a passage of In Search of Bisco that this might be true, stipulating of course that the blacks do work harder.

Caldwell presents the progeny of slaves and the

the slave work-status in a revealing array of jobs. Introduced as they were into a plantation society, the blacks had
predominantly agricultural jobs, and they are often seen in
such work in Caldwell's writings. In the mid-1930's the
black fieldhands, producing the basic crop, cotton, were
getting 75 cents and later a dollar a day. The work was
for the blacks; the cotton was for the whites. On various
farms in various works, blacks were engaged in plowing and
cultivating. In one book, a black is seen plowing with mules,
while whites are working with tractors (A House in the Uplands). Commonly, the white farmer, as for example Clay
Horey in Journeyman, limits his work to getting the blacks
started on time in the fields. In God's Little Acre, two
blacks especially, Black Sam and Uncle Felix, are continually present. The only crops produced are raised by the
blacks. In addition to plowing and cultivating, the blacks
also help to dig for gold and do general excavation work.
Black Sam also washes dishes, and Uncle Felix guards the
albino.

    In Journeyman, a black shucking corn is the first
person encountered on a farm. He is sent to fetch the
owner; or he can direct visitors to whichever pasture the
owner is in. When a jug of liquor is wanted, the black
man goes for it. Several ever-present farm hands are
constantly being called on to report what they have witnessed.
Hunnicutt Branch is thus crucial to the mechanics of "Hamrick's Polar Bear." Any odd job, like carrying the body of
a mother-in-law into the house, may be expected to be done
by blacks. Such workers might be on a place for fifty years,
as reported by In Search of Bisco, and, when no longer able
to function effectively, be evicted. In addition to not being
eligible for social security when overtaken by age, these
workers have been replaced by machinery and itinerant
Mexicans. In the Sixties, a rice farmer in Arkansas, having
a strong antipathy to blacks, reports his pleasure that the
use of machinery has caused all blacks to be sent away.
He expresses fear of lawlessness in blacks and is glad they
are gone.

    In You Have Seen Their Faces mention is made of the
fact that some blacks do have farms of their own. One has
37 acres near Ripley, Tennessee, a place he has bought for
$1800 on time as opposed to the $1100 cash it would have
cost. He has no idea how much he has paid and does not
expect to pay it off. Though he is better off than most

blacks, he hates to farm such worn-out land. He has no
where else to turn.

In Miss Mama Aimée the statement is made that the
"ordinary" black people do all the servant work. As has
been true throughout the ages, body servants come to be
very influential, though the blacks walk a chalk line of sub-
servience at the same time. Sam Moxley of Jenny by Nature
(1961) and Wardlow of Trouble in July (1940) are very similar in their relationships to two politically-minded judges.
Sam cooks meals, makes the judge's bed, presses his pants,
and generally runs his life. Gentle, soft-spoken, widowed,
sixtyishly-energetic, he has devoted his life to caring for
the house, the garden, and the judge. He goes to the house
of Jenny and interrupts the love-making of the judge against
his will and complaint, dressing him and taking him home.
He says he promised to do his duty and he is doing it.
The judge sheepishly allows himself to be led home, like a
wayward child. When the judge finally decides to marry,
Sam successfully stipulates that his orders concerning the
household and other duties will be relayed to him through
the judge.

Wardlow has less prestige. Zerena White, of The
Earnshaw Neighborhood (1971), has a great deal more.
She consistently supplies limitation to the ideas of the
woman she works for and feels free to comment openly on
what she does. She happily and successfully supports her
daughter's decision not to wear a uniform to work. Naturally, the households develop a dependence on long-time
domestic servants, particularly cooks. Miss Mama Aimée
cries when Martha gets disgusted and announces she is
leaving; she will be hard to replace. The position of a
cook, or maid, or household servant is strategic in A
House in the Uplands, Close to Home, and Place Called
Estherville. A cook plays an important role in the action
of Episode in Palmetto. In Around About America (1964)
it was noted that the chef who came out of the kitchen of
a New Orleans restaurant to accept compliments on his
gumbo was black.

The blacks are, of course, everywhere and all-
knowing. They are portrayed by Caldwell as being all-
purpose small problem solvers. Como, the black porter
in "Martha Jean," intends to sleep by the fire at "Nick's
Place" instead of going home, where it is cold. In just a

few pages, he puts a shovel of coal on the fire, closes the
door to the place, helps with drinks and sandwiches, gets
another shovel of coal, is ordered to get sandwiches and
coffee, gets a slice of cake on order, is called a "shoeshine African," prepares a room upstairs, is called upon
(but knows better than to respond) for assistance by a
young woman, is ordered to throw the narrator of the story
out, advances fearfully as though to do it, throws another
hod of coal on the fire, and puts out the light.

    Similarly, two blacks, Sam and Amos, provide the
engine for "Meddlesome Jack." In spite of themselves,
they, because they do not have sufficient personality status
to separate themselves from the situation, go through a
series of grotesque maneuvers with the jackass, which has
an unsettling effect on women. The blacks in this case
blunder through their fear of both the animal and the whites.
Amos has inadvertently traded a dollar watch for a very
troublesome animal. He is ordered to handle the animal,
which has transfixed him. The white man for whom he
works gives him a series of orders which he is not able
to carry out, being afraid.

    Beckum and Bisco are tattered ten-year-olds who
serve as general servants about the main establishment of
A House in the Uplands. They sweep up the yard, take the
the heads off chickens, look for money dropped through
cracks in the veranda, scrounge puffs from cigarette butts,
lick drops out of discarded whiskey bottles, sound the bell
for dinner, and watch the meal being served. They are
always at hand, even to climbing the porch columns and
watching what is going on in lighted rooms for hours at a
time. Of much higher status is Lee, the large, muscular,
twenty-year-old houseboy at a roadhouse in The Last Night
of Summer (1963). At nightfall he switches on the sign
advertising beer and switches it off at daylight. He cares
for the lawn and removes trash from the front of the place.
Lee also has continually to turn away tourists who have
lost their way and have mistaken the establishment for a
motel rather than a whore house. He never loses his temper and patiently counters allegations that there should be
a lighted sign indicating there are no vacancies by saying
a recent windstorm destroyed it. He points the way to the
main highway where they can look for what they want. In
addition to being the bouncer when needed, he takes care
of ice, soft drinks, and liquor. He also prepares a special

Leeburger, which contains marijuana.

The most commonly encountered general-purpose
assignment is that of yard-boy. In Search of Bisco lists
the following duties for a typical yardboy in his dawn-to-
lights-out day: sweeping the porches, hosing the garden,
cleaning the privy, butchering a hog, plucking a chicken,
splitting firewood, raking leaves, and saddling a horse, as
well as a number of household chores, and in fact anything
the master or mistress of the house may think of--which
might include arranging sexual exhibitions of young black
men or the procuring of a black girl for the sexual enjoyment of whites. Georgia Boy (1943) is devoted to a
teenage yardboy, Handsome Brown, whose preposterous ad-
ventures in the ridiculous Stroup family are a presentation
of horseplay by a naive narrator for the purpose of expression of indignation against a maladjusted world. At the
same time it appears to be superficially an amusing set of
anecdotes and has often been taken as such.

Handsome spends his time in the no-man's-land between the warring Mr. and Mrs. Stroup. She is nobody's
bargain, and he is a ne'er-do-well and a nincompoop. Handsome is not particularly intelligent, but he is a cut above
the two he has to serve. The book details one outrageous
imposition after another on Handsome. He has constantly
to meet the conflicting demands of the Stroups without excuse or complaint and never gets to use his own common
sense. He has to embark on ridiculous projects and silently
take the blame. He often has to stand for being second-
guessed by the person who forced him into a foolish under-
taking, usually Morris Stroup. Though the constant barrage
of dire threats against him is empty, they represent a steady
environment of harassment. He is, in short, the focus of
the complete inadequacy of the Stroups.

His pay, like that of all the other yardboys, is minimal. He eats leftovers, sleeps in the barn, and is given
hand-me-downs occasionally. He has just barely heard of
money. He theoretically has a day off, but he is always
wanted for some other duty when he asks for it. In addition to
being given sleeveless tasks to perform, he even has to
put up with being told that Mr. Stroup, whose only work is
to avoid work, never has a day off. He is the very type of
exploitation without recourse. The discards given to Handsome Brown were more common than pay of a few dollars

weekly. The most Christian of ladies were cunning and
merciless in their maneuvering of their help into lesser
rewards. If any complaint was made about lack of payment
or of a failure to keep a pay agreement, the threat of jail
for non-payment of fictitious debt or on some other false
charge was invoked. The court could be depended upon to
accept the word of a white as opposed to that of a black.
The situations of such persons were portrayed by Caldwell
in a state of rage tempered by compassion for those who
did not know how to escape their situations.

        Because blacks had been brought into society as con-
veniences to the whites, they generally had the status of
readily-available, all-purpose help whom any white can call
upon. In A House in the Uplands, when there was a hard
rain, blacks were pressed into service to go through the
house putting every available container in place to catch
water from roof leaks. When a group of men go camping
in Summer Island, a black is taken along to help. In
"Daughter" a black is sent with a message to the landowner,
and another is handed the reins of the team hauling a load
of cotton so the driver can join an accumulating crowd.
When fish respond too plentifully, a passing black boy is
paid a quarter to help handle them (Close to Home). A
widow gives a small black boy a nickel at intervals to rake
her trash up into a pile (The Sure Hand of God). In
Trouble in July, the sheriff, who goes fishing to avoid involvement in a lynching, plans to find a black to do his
cooking when he gets to the river. A ferocious white, who
has killed several blacks, presses blacks into service to
look for his wife, who has fallen into a well (Trouble in
July). Even though Zerena, in The Earnshaw Neighborhood,
is able to organize and present her claims effectively, she
is not able to stop the people she worked for from care-
lessly dropping newspapers on the floor.

        As has already been suggested, blacks appear in
Caldwell's pages in a variety of low-level jobs. They do
most of the work at a sawmill, help to shore up the under-
mined house in God's Little Acre, carry firewood, haul
logs, shine shoes, provide maid service, wash dishes,
move household goods, perform guard duty, tow tractors,
drive wagons, and help mechanics. Along with a group of
elevator operators and porters, there are a bartender and
a waiter. The only barber is unemployed. A bell boy is
also a pimp. A truck driver goes to Florida for oranges;

another is allowed to go to a nearby city, unload, and hurry
back to the plantation. The only black in a court is the
judge's janitor. Though Caldwell points out that whites have,
ironically, a deep interest in black entertainment (In Search
of Bisco), he portrays only three black musicians. They
play piano, horns, and drums in The White Turkey, a
brothel. They pick up the coins after the muff-dancer has
finished her act (Tragic Ground). A story, "Runaway,"
deals with the nine-year-old black girl who is living as
the over-worked servant of whites. Finally she leaves and
returns to the protection of blacks, who defend and keep
her.

    The great majority of black workers, when Caldwell
was portraying them in Some American People (1935) and
You Have Seen Their Faces (1937), were either sharecroppers
or tenant farmers. The system under which they lived, variously administered from place to place, was thought of as
being as close to the situation of slavery as possible. Both
blacks and whites were involved, though the whites were
being displaced by blacks because of the whites' greater
vulnerability. Caldwell thought that blacks, performing the
same tasks as formerly, were worse off than a half-century
before. Additionally, they had the envy and anger of the
poor whites, whom they displaced. Blacks often earned
more than whites, perhaps $200 annually as opposed to $100.
Because they were easier to suppress, the blacks, though
slightly better-paid, had inferior housing, education, and
health. Not only was it cheaper that way; the ignorance
and deprivation made for better control. Caldwell notes
that sharecropper families were usually black and usually
large.

    Caldwell captured his view of the renting black farm
worker in "The End of Christy Tucker." Tucker has been
summoned to appear before the landowner. He has moved
from Alabama to Georgia because he wanted to progress.
He has no idea what the owner wants but does think this
will be an opportunity to ask for more equipment. His attitude suggests that black workers often have only a vague
idea of the system in which they are trapped. Tucker soon
perceives that he is on the carpet, though he has no sense
of wrong-doing. This is part of his crime, being "biggity,"
a term still used in the South. He had bought a radio elsewhere than at the plantation store. He naively explains that
he got a better deal elsewhere and did not want to go into

debt to the plantation store. He has replaced pickets in a
fence without permission. His wife has raised chickens
without permission. He has trapped rabbits without permission. He says he has to get things done. The owner
judges him guilty of acting as though he thought he was as
good as a white man. Emphasizing the complete absence of
economic rights of the tenant, the owner tells him it is
none of his business how his account stands.

    As punishment for his stepping out of his prescribed
subservient role, Tucker is told to kneel on the floor and
allow himself to be strapped. He refuses to accept the
unwarranged punishment and its juvenile character. He is
struck once, grabs the strap, refuses to let go, and is shot
three times and killed. The owner's brother and the book-
keeper are ready to testify that the owner shot in self-
defense. There would, of course, be no trial. When Caldwell looks for Bisco, thirty years later, another black thinks
he got into trouble for talking too freely and had to go
away--he had complained that he was not paid all the money
due him and left rather than make the mistake of fighting.
Caldwell points out that the tenant was constantly reminded
of the effects of knife, rifle, and fire.

    In You Have Seen Their Faces, Caldwell gives a
summary of an actual counterpart of Christy Tucker: no
matter how good his crops, no matter how much he actually
produces, he owes money at the end of the year. The
books are rigged. He can buy only at his plantation store.
If he takes the trouble to walk to another, it will be the
property of another planter, who will report his actions so
that he can be summoned to give a reason for his violation.
If he is sick, his weekly credit will be cut from $4.50 to
$3.50. All medical bills will be charged against his
account. He lives with his grandmother. If she dies, he
will have to marry, for each cabin must supply at least one
worker. On some plantations, workers receive coupons instead of money. No tenant can leave without permission,
which is only granted upon payment of a lump sum to liqui-
date a constantly-mentioned and unstipulated "back debt."
The amount of the debt is always more than the meager
amount of cash a worker can accumulate. Thus anyone who
tries to leave can be arrested for debt. A general punishment for transgression is a whipping administered by a man
on horseback.

    As suggested earlier, a few managed to achieve a

form of farm ownership. Ambitious people who want to
think or work for themselves can expect some form of the
Christy Tucker treatment. Many workers were, through
inadequate compensation and bogus charges, forced gradually
from sharecropper to renter to wage-hand, each stage being
less advantageous. The latter had only the uncertain promise
of ten dollars each for the few months when the field work
was carried on. Caldwell points out in Some American
People (1935) that strangers who travel through the country
and study conditions are watched and, if necessary, escorted
from the area and intimidated. This still was his observation when he wrote The Weather Shelter (1969).

In spite of the repressive circumstances just described,
blacks did move away from the South, particularly under the
impact of World War II. And they tried to move up as well
as away. Caldwell portrays through Duke Hopkins what
might happen to a black who wants to achieve the status of
a professional in Summertime Island (1968). Duke, muscular and in his early twenties, had attended a segregated
high school and college in Kentucky and now teaches geography and history in a black high school. His salary is so
low that, though single, he has to run a barber shop in off-
hours. Product of a racial mixture, he has brown, wavy
hair, freckles, and blue eyes.

In the novel, Caldwell takes him through a series of
circumstances designed to show the tortuous path of the
educated black as he encounters the ignorant bigotry still
existing in southern towns. He suggests there is a great
middle body of placidly shocked whites which may eventually
be moved to modest action. Generally, in this novel, they
stand as disapproving bystanders who are afraid to curb the
offender. The culmination of Duke's struggle against his
nemesis, a red-neck, feisty ignoramus, is that the man,
whose repression Duke has resisted, rams him with his
truck, hospitalizing him. The white who is the voice of
decency says he will collect money for Duke's hospital ex-
penses and discontinue his association with the offender.
There is no thought of punishment for the criminal behavior.

Caldwell captures all the elements he feels must be
in the mind of Duke, who is obviously both deeply sensitive
and pressured, in a sleep-talking session. His conversation covers a dozen factors: (1) the lack of mercy of the
whites; (2) the sense of the restraint under which he con-

stantly lives; (3) the indignity of the pretense that he was
an Indian by a woman who wanted him; (4) his insistence
on the fact of his heritage; (5) the necessity of constantly
running from danger; (6) the barrage of peremptory commands; (7) the necessity of responding courteously to arbi-
trary commands; (8) the danger to black men represented
by white women; (9) the especial danger related to white
female nakedness; (10) the danger of immediate execution
if problems related to white female nakedness arose; (11)
his desire to live a life as unencumbered as that of anyone
else; and (12) a plea to white women to realize their danger
to black men.

Conditioned as it is by the very real threat of the
aggressive actions of a white woman with a strong sexual
interest in him, the list is longer than it might be.   Duke
is young.   The possibilities of life to his trained mind are
many.   But he sees that inferior people can destroy his
potential for ironic and frustrating reasons.   Caldwell causes
him to be injured rather than killed.   The writer mentioned
to Caldwell that he hated having Duke run down by the insecure bigot.   "It had to be, " he said, meaning that we may
expect educated blacks to be subjected to such destructive
acts, not to mention the other demeaning elements which
are played out in the book.   Getting blacks into schools will
not be enough, he seems to be saying.   We shall also have
to see that society has a place for them after they have
worked to achieve their skills and formulated their aspira-
tions.   He sees that we cannot on the one hand ask blacks
to aspire and on the other degrade them in a way that was
so essential to their economic exploitation.

On a subject allied to this, the black in business,
Caldwell makes virtually no observations, the only item
being his inclusion of a bait shop owner of Augusta, Georgia,
in You Have Seen Their Faces.   Possibly this is because
he has not been aware of many blacks in business.   The
matter of the way employment involves racial integration
is touched.   The major phenomenon of black occupational
acceptance has been in the realm of entertainment.   As
early as in Poor Fool (1930), Caldwell had a black fighter,
Knockout Harris, accepted by the crowd as soon as he overcame his white opponent.   In this brutal arena, the one who
could provide the desired excitement would get the reward.
The acceptance would not necessarily be extended to social
considerations, of course.   In Tragic Ground (1944) a poor

white of modest capability was replaced in a war plant by
a strong black. In The Bastard (1929) it was noted that
the laborers in the seed mill, who were both white and
black, gambled together. When he wrote Call It Experience
(1951), he recalled there was no color line in the labor gang
of the feed mill where he worked in the town of Wrens,
Georgia. The racial discrimination was, of course, operative away from the mill. In The Weather Shelter, Caldwell
caused an enlightened owner of a pony farm to have black
and white exercise boys work together.

          A factor allied to the struggle that blacks, in Cald-
well's works and elsewhere, had and have for congenial
employment is that they have consistently been given minimal
economic satisfaction in their work. Black poverty did not
just happen, nor was it desired: it is a calculated product
of the pattern of manipulation of blacks for the economic
advantage of their employers. Caldwell displays continually
a distinct interest in the limited rewards of the black workers as late as In Search of Bisco; he maintains that pre-
venting the black from working in a rewarding occupation or
profession has been and is by design. The workers whose
efforts made possible the wealth of the plantations, kept to
a limited range of jobs with a minimum of reward, have
continually lived in places like "Needmore" in Trouble in
July--so named, it is explained, because the blacks were
always told in the stores there that they would need more
money than they had. In "Medicine Man" most of the members of the original audience of the show were blacks with
no money. They stepped aside when the real customers
appeared. The blacks sniffed wistfully at the alcohol fumes
from the patent medicine.

          A section of "Tracing Life with a Finger," dating
from about 1930, suggests Caldwell's memory of his father's
benevolence to the poor, black or white. After the fictional
father points out to his son blacks who have only cornbread
made with water to eat, the youth steals from the family
pantry to take to the family. In A House in the Uplands he
explores in a scene between a landowner and an aged black
worker one phase of the relationship between poverty and
systematic and callous economic suppression. The man
has worked for sixty years on one farm. His pay has been
an occasional handout and bed and board. His son has returned from the army and lives in a nearby town, where he
works in a mill. He wants his parents to live with him.

The owner stipulates that the worker and his wife will have
to pay five hundred dollars before they can leave. The
wife is not allowed to go separately, either. The owner's
statements are made in arrogant and threatening terms.

As a counterfoil and as an indication that other forces
are at work in that society, the owner's cousin, a lawyer,
appears and suggests that letting the man and his wife go
would be the decent thing to do. But the owner, irrelevantly
and emotionally, says no black is going to tell him what to
do. He says that people like his cousin, if successful,
would cause all the white women to be raped and all the
white men to be shot, for the freedom would set the blacks
wild. He feels that talk of fundamental rights for blacks
undoes all that has been established in the last century.
To add to the irony of the situation, Caldwell has a poor
white farmer say that a black cannot disobey a white, no
matter what he says. No matter how unjust the amount
asked, the black will have to pay the money. The poor
white is perfectly capable of resenting the fact that not only
is he displaced by a black but he is as well reinforcing
the mad system which makes it possible.

Throughout his work, Caldwell gives glimpses of
the penury of blacks. A woman, sitting in a house which
has a chair with a cement sack for a back and a fringe of
newspaper over the mantel of the fireplace, says the chickens
have eaten all the corn. A black girl standing beside the
wasted body of her brother says he just began to shrivel
eleven years earlier. There is no suggestion of being able
to get medical assistance. An aged black woman, holding
a skillet over a fire, says her man would like some meat
to go with the cornbread. As late as In Search of Bisco,
Caldwell mentions that, back off the road, the blacks are
still in enforced poverty. He writes of the rats which go
with poverty.

Poverty of the blacks is mirrored in common phrases
used by various characters. The owner in A House in the
Uplands is ruined: a by-stander notes that he is probably
as bad off as a black after Saturday night. In "Honeymoon"
it is suggested that, on the occasion of a projected ex-
tremity, he will be ready to give the place to the blacks and
the weevils. The equality of status of the worst insect ever
known to the cotton farmer and his most important tool is
ironic but not accidental. Similarly, a farm in "The Growing

Season" is so bad that all the blacks, who would work even
the most barren land as long as possible, are gone.   In
God's Little Acre, the blacks are constantly asking for
something to eat.   Black Sam even threatens to butcher the
mule.   There is no sympathy.   One of the annoying circumstances a farmer mentioned is that the blacks eat the
watermelons as soon as they are ripe.   No mention is made
of how they are starved because of non-existent recompense.

   Economic discrimination is reported in Some American
People as existing even on the relief projects.   The black
works longer for his pay than the white, who supervises.
Also, the blacks are given less desirable food and may be
charged for what was to be distributed free.   Loans are at
exorbitant rates.   In You Have Seen Their Faces, a picture
shows blacks lined up for monthly pension checks of four
dollars.   Additional kinds of economic discrimination, all
aimed at driving down the black standard of living, were
still operative when In Search of Bisco was written.   Employees in a small town, where a boycott of an offender is
effective, are much more subservient to wishes of employers
than when competition for services is greater.   The lack of
employment protection produces acquiescent workers who
have to accept less pay.   Housewives are as bad as the
businessmen--they employ on a short term to avoid paying
the social security tax.   A woman from New England,
living in Louisiana, found herself ostracized by her neighbors.   The reason was that she paid her maid extra for
extra work.   In retribution, gossip about her morality was
circulated.   As reflected in Caldwell's works, the climate
of work done by blacks may be expected to be one of harassment.   A black waiter at a country club (The Last Night of
Summer) is subjected by a woman to abusive remarks about
his color and about losing his job when she orders a drink,
jerking at the waiter's towel while ordering and then grabbing
the drink when it arrives.   A white waiter could not be
expected to tolerate such treatment, but a black one maintains a necessary icy calm.

   The matter of physical brutality is much more not-
able, of course.   Caldwell's In Search of Bisco says that
the beatings which used to be administered as punishment
for faulty work, non-payment of debt, or claiming to be sick
and not working, are no longer in evidence.   But he has
vividly pictured those methods that transcend minor physical
punishment, like withholding money or food or clothing.   In

Close to Home it is noted that no white man has ever been brought to trial in the county in question for killing a black. The situation is always like that of Christy Tucker. Sometimes the whites killed in terms of violent confrontation.

The most vicious example of killing on general principles of submission is found in The Bastard. The operator of a sawmill, noting that the black laborers are eating watermelon, threateningly orders the men to stop eating and get back to work. One of the men takes a last handful and stuffs it into his mouth as he goes back to his machine. Cursing, the operator clubs him across the head and again across the face. The unconscious man is ripped by his saw. The sadistic operator goes for a crowbar and hits the head of the corpse several times. The body had been partially bisected at the waist by the saw. The owner finishes cutting the body into two pieces on the saw. The owner explains to a friend that there is nothing to worry about; blacks are always getting killed by the saw. He sawed one up laterally the year before. The two parts of the body are taken to the worker's cabin and dumped there. The atmosphere of the whole episode is one of desperate sadism, motivated by unrecognized fear. In Trouble in July a white tenant farmer is known to have killed a black for breaking a hoe handle and another for a significantly-unidentified lesser cause.

In Close to Home mention is made of the fact that not all whites approve of gratuitous killings, other outrageous punishments, and generalized terrorism in the interest of repression. Some whites feel shame when they hear of flogging for leaving work early or being shot for tardy repayment of a small debt. They do not believe in mistreatment of animals, either, Caldwell sarcastically causes his speaker to add.

Caldwell uses a brother and a sister in Place Called Estherville to illustrate problems of employment. Kathyanne leaves one house where her employer's husband forces her sexual submission. She knows it will do no good to say anything about it. Having lost that job, she works for a woman who is socially acceptable but so unscrupulous as to expect her to accept payment in used clothes. Evidently there had not been an agreement on a specified amount of money, but Kathyanne has to point out the obvious, that she has to pay her rent in cash. The employer then mentions

the duty of whites to give advice to innocent and incompetent
blacks.   When Kathyanne rejects the clothes in place of
cash and says she will just have to find a job which does
pay money, the woman becomes angry and indignant.   She
takes the position that such things as falling behind in rent
are the result of racial inadequacy.   Then she says that
she has long wanted to say she has a deep hatred for noxious
blacks.   She has shifted her humiliation and rage at not
really being able to afford a servant to the most immediate
object, one which cannot fight back.   The woman threatens
to keep her from all other employment if she quits.   She
will say that Kathyanne is like all the rest of her race:
thieving, lying, immoral.   Kathyanne says with dignity,
come what may, she will just have to manage.   She could
never work for her after that.   When Kathyanne leaves,
the employer is begging her to promise that she will not
tell people that she was asked to work for castoffs.   But
she leaves determinedly without doing so.

     Ganus, Kathyanne's brother, a delivery boy, falls
into the clutches of a grass widow who finds him desirable.
After trying to avoid making deliveries to her, and eluding
her twice, he succumbs to her embrace, for the first time
forgetting entirely about skin color.   It would have been
impossible for him to tell his white employer that a white
woman wanted him.   Because he needs the job, he has to
knowingly and helplessly pursue his own doom: eventually a
white woman falsely claims molestation, a common element
in Caldwell plots, and this causes Ganus' death.

     The factors, not all as exciting and momentarily
pleasant as being wanted sexually, which relate to deteriora-
tion of the employment situation of blacks are like the series
of pressures in guerrilla warfare.   A black sharecropper who
follows rules set by the whites, it is observed in You Have
Seen Their Faces, can live a peaceful life.   One who so
much as argues about the number of bales raised will be
dogged as long as he lives, however.   In Search of Bisco
has an account of a black veteran who had become thoroughly
qualified as a truck driver while in the service.   His color
has made it impossible to get anything more than jobs hauling trash or part-time work in a filling station.   Trucking
companies say they cannot risk problems relating to segregation in dining and sleeping accommodations on the road.
A black driver jailed on a trumped-up charge would cause
costly delay on the road.   These limitations have no

relationship to the man's own conduct but are very real.

It may be observed that the role of the black, especially in the crucial matter of employment, is that of
scapegoat. Blacks, usually in lower levels of authority,
are an easily-available and undefended butt for the frustra-
tions of those in control of their work or on a higher social
or economic level. Somewhat witlessly, an employer in a
state of agitation will blame the breaking of a plate on a
maid (Close to Home). A truck driver dislikes everything
a black teacher does, including the way he makes coffee,
desperately trying to assert superiority (Summertime Island).
A high school graduate notices that he is more receptive to
blacks then some one that did not complete the elementary
grades. He has stumbled, without knowing it, into the reason of all the abuse of blacks by whites, their desperate
need to release the tension of their own guilt and inadequacy.
Neither the blacks nor the whites know why the black scapegoat is so crucially important to the ignorant and needy
whites. As suggested before, Caldwell has devoted a whole
book, Georgia Boy, to this relationship. It would not be
like Caldwell to analyze the psychological structure of the
relationship. But it is very clearly delineated. Though the
book is generally thought of as humorous and full of fantastic situations, the real incongruity is between what is and
what ought to be. And it is right on the target of the relationship between the white exploiters and the deprived
blacks, struggling for consciousness and competence to meet
the situation.

The exploitation of the black consumer has been suggested already but was outlined further by Caldwell. Though
the whites want the blacks to work for as little as possible
at a limited range of jobs, the white merchants want whatever money the blacks get. It will be recalled that the
plantation owners inform on blacks who go out of their own
area. The general idea is to keep as complete control of
the individual black's funds or credit as possible. Not only
did the whites want to control funds, but they also wanted
to be in a position to make up false accounts. In the matter
of blacks who wanted to leave farms, the device of con-
veniently-arranged "debts" was important. One of the advantages of having black workers was that they were less
likely to be able to question the one-sided bookkeeping methods of the owners. In A House in the Uplands mention is
made of the fact that the last man to leave without paying

the arbitrarily-derived debt was sentenced to ten years on
a chain gang. A preposterous list of his supposed debts
includes payment for the loss of a mule which had killed
itself by ramming its head against a tree. The white who
relates the case intends it to be a lesson for listening blacks.
When Handsome Brown has supposedly run away, Mrs.
Stroup takes the occasion to belabor Mr. Stroup for having
forced an unprepared black out into the world, where he is
certain to come to grief. Stroup replies that running away
was wrong, no matter how great the provocation. He considers it to be illegal for a black to leave without asking
permission. Indeed, he might have owed some money.
And it is apparent that a request to leave would have re-
sulted in the discovery of a debt, no matter how bizarre
the derivation of it might be.

In Trouble in July, a man says it is time to put
pressure on the blacks again, the kind of attitude that would
lead to a lynching, for example. He has seen a black in a
store with more money than any white. Keeping all blacks
automatically at a lower status than all whites was very
important to the less fortunate or less capable whites.
The poverty of spirit which made that position attractive
excused another generally accepted idea--that cheating
blacks was the sensible and natural thing to do, sort of
like picking berries that might grow in the field. Otherwise,
it would be like letting an opportunity go to waste.

In Summertime Island, in discussing his ultimate
red-necked ignoramus, Caldwell says these are the kind of
people who cheat the blacks. They short-weight them in
crop shares of corn or cotton. They continually cheat them
at stores. In Search of Bisco mentions installment collec-
tors who threaten to call the police if they are not over-
paid. Usually the blacks, whose experience has not led
them to expect fair treatment from the police, pay rather
than seek further trouble. Pseudo-salesmen take down-
payments and are never heard from again. Mrs. Stroup
includes in her accusations of her husband that he cheated
an orphan black boy who was afraid to speak up for his
rights. Stroup's son adds that his father even cheats Handsome at marbles. The case of Ganus in Place Called Estherville is a full exploitation of collusive cheating of a black
teenager by a bicycle shop owner and a doctor. The youth
needs a bicycle so that he can take a job as a delivery boy.
Naturally, he has no money. The doctor, whose office has

at least as much traffic from his operations as a loan shark
as from his function as a physician, arranges to finance him
in the matter. The basic price of the wheel is $49.50.
The shop owner pressures him into several unneeded extras.
The loan is financed at $5 per week for six months, for a
total of $120. When Ganus loses his job, the bicycle is
repossessed with no refund.

The black dollar is just as good as any other. One
difference in black trade is that ethics are completely forgotten, mainly because there is nothing to require them to
be remembered. Another is that the black customer's presence is not as desirable as the money. A black customer
is not supposed to linger after a purchase. In Summertime
Island a storekeeper objects to a black staying in a store
after a purchase is made. He is with whites who prepare
to munch on cheese and crackers they have bought. The
white owner does not propose to have a black chew in front
of him. It was Erskine's father, the Rev. I. S. Caldwell,
who wrote a letter to a New York newspaper to comment
on The Little Foxes. A woman of the class and type of
Mrs. Hubbard, he pointed out, would not ask a servant
either white or black to eat cakes in the living room in
the presence of guests.

The same kind of person who makes it a policy to
"cheat hell" out of blacks in The Weather Shelter can also
believe in segregated businesses and segregation within
businesses. Some merchandise (Deep South) can be expected
to be marked for whites only. When blacks are allowed to
try on shoes or clothing, such a person will believe, the
merchandise is ruined for whites. And it is certain that
the majority of the whites Caldwell was writing about would
agree. What is true in regard to trade with blacks is also
true in relation to housing. Though much consideration has
been given to remedying the matter of segregated housing
over the years, particularly in the last decade or so, the
pattern across the country is still one of segregated areas
for blacks. And that is certainly what Caldwell describes
in all his works. Even the black and white sharecroppers
are segregated, as in Deep South. The significance of the
segregation is most important in regard to the desirability
of the area involved. In Search of Bisco refers to the fact
that whites commonly live on high ground and blacks, in
the country or on low ground beside the walls or railroads.
Whites will have paved streets when blacks have paths; the

whites' houses may be compared to less-elaborate, substandard houses, or even shacks.   In The Earnshaw Neighborhood (1971) Caldwell refers to Roysterville and its relation to the black section, Dingy Flats: the whites are
moving into areas where restrictions are based on size and
value of house rather than color.   The blacks have moved
into this southern town from the country and are raising
large families.   They have spread beyond the original Dingy
Flats.   The whites keep moving to separate themselves from
the spreading blacks.   Near Dingy Flats there is said to be
the threat of property damage and the occasion for association with blacks in public places.

        In Close to Home, the town jail has been completely
surrounded by the black area.   Streets are curbless and are
not maintained.   One has to avoid mudholes and fallen trees
in traveling them.   The Weather Shelter describes the area
where blacks live in the same way.   Caldwell notes in Miss
Mama Aimée that the black area has difficulty in getting
people to come and make repairs.   In Tragic Ground,
reference is made to Poor Boy, which is such a bad section that even the blacks and Mexicans could not be induced
to live there.   As they travel about the country, both Caldwell and his wife continue to note the character of housing.
In March 1971, in Florida, she noted "pitiful" shacks in-
habited by blacks, right next to the road, with large holes
in the siding and roof.   On the farm, Caldwell notes the
same segregation.   In Journeyman there is a group of
cabins several hundred yards away from Clay Horey's farm-
house.   The cabins with many children about are mentioned
in Summertime Island.   In Some American People (1935),
a white tenant has moved into a cabin from which a black
has recently been evicted.   It is believed that the black
family found a home in a roofless, abandoned barn some
miles away.   In Deep South (1968) a destitute white with
eleven children has moved into a shack abandoned by blacks.

        In You Have Seen Their Faces Caldwell takes pains
to say how limited the black cabins on some farms are.
In Marion Junction, Alabama, the camera found a black
cabin with cotton growing right up to it.   The captain says
that the overseer allows no ground to be taken up by a
garden, cotton being the overwhelming factor.   Elsewhere
pictures of two cabins of blacks are accompanied by the
notation that the owner has agreed to allow the attachment

of numerous tobacco and patent medicine signs to the meager
building. As late as In Search of Bisco (1965), Caldwell
was noting that it was a legitimate part of a person's estate
to have a few houses in the black quarter. The owner of
substandard houses in the area enforcedly occupied by the
blacks would believe that the blacks could afford no better.
He may not be expected to ask why their incomes are low.
He knows that the real estate men are pledged to keep
blacks out of the white area of town, no matter how much
they earn. Any black who placed the highest bid on a home
would be submitted to intense and concentrated pressure.
Such a person could be reminded that the blacks have a
night a week at the drive-in. That privilege could be with-
drawn.

        In Agricola (The Sure Hand of God, 1947), one of
the wealthiest men gets most of his income from the rental
of sixty or seventy shanties in the black quarter. He does
not have to supply water, as he would for whites, and does
not have to make repairs, because blacks are afraid to ask
for them. They are afraid that he will evict them, leaving
them with no place to live, because they may not live outside the designated area. In Place Called Estherville (1949),
Caldwell shows the same economic squeeze through the visit
of a rent collector to a black tenant, who does not have the
money. The renter is an attractive black girl, who has
twice been forced to submit sexually to whites. She still
does not want to. Her black friend, who has to accept her
pregnancy by the white man because he loves her (and does
eventually marry her), aggressively tells the collector,
rather ambiguously, that whites should leave blacks alone.
The collector neglects his fiscal duty because he has a
combined desire to help her and take advantage of her.
He wants to trade the rent money for sex. In this case,
she faces him down, and he is sufficiently shaken that he
writes her a receipt for the rent, though he has received
neither money nor favors. The episode suggests one of the
many ways the lever of segregated housing has been used
to squeeze the black tenants.

        Repression is an instrument of economic manipula-
tion. The difference between the depleted poor whites, whom
their users continually bribe by bogus appeals to their thread-
bare pride, and the blacks is that the whites have social mo-
bility. But, through segregation, the blacks are locked in

place, locationally and occupationally. Part of that difference which has saved the poor whites for the incumbent
white political and economic structure has been the battery
of physical manifestations. In <u>Summertime Island,</u> elderly
blacks are peremptorily ordered to stand up at the approach
of whites. Thus in <u>You Have Seen Their Faces</u> one reads
that removal of hats on seeing a white near is common.
The only black to be seen around a courtroom in <u>A House
in the Uplands</u> is the janitor. He stops sweeping and bows
deeply to one of the lawyers.

When he was asked about his portrayal of sheriffs,
which is anything but flattering, Caldwell said that penal
institutions in small towns were very primitive. There
were usually two cells for the purpose of racial segregation. "I was very unhappy about the treatment of prisoners.
Talks with Negroes always ended up with the fact that their
troubles began with not stepping off the sidewalk." The law
enforcement people had "no human feelings at all," he
thought. The degradation which was a part of control and
repression could only be achieved in the absence of an
adequate legal system. Two instances will suffice to show
how Caldwell suggests that degradation. There is nothing
peculiar about the sexual degradation of women. It has
been going on for a long time. But a very significant part
of the white attitude, portrayed by Caldwell, toward blacks
is that male whites considered it was constantly open season on female blacks. Perhaps consequently, the most inflammatory consideration for whites was intercourse between
a black male and a white female, especially forcibly (it
would appear to be the normal attitude of whites that no
white woman would offer herself to a black).

The foregoing considerations are offered to highlight
the sexual degradation of Kathyanne in <u>Place Called Esther-
ville</u> (1949). A businessman has some visiting buyers from
Atlanta in his little town; they obviously are expecting sexual
entertainment. He has never been put in this situation before, but he is nerved to the task by the conviction that he
will lose their business if he does not produce. Kathyanne
had been picked up, for no reason, by the town constable,
who was trying to gain her sexual favors by letting her go.
Instead, her fine had been paid by the businessman, who
was making a certain kind of investment. Kathyanne laughs
when she realizes that the man has come to see her for
sexual purposes. But she feels trapped and succumbs silently

after finding he has paid her fine. She expresses her hatred
of all white men and her wish that they would leave the
blacks alone. She is taken into a car and out into the night
for the enjoyment of at least two of the three men. The extent to which the judicial system as recorded by Caldwell
would make a black feel cornered is suggested by the fact
that the girl was not even allowed to know who had paid her
fine after her unjust arrest.

In "Blue Boy, " Caldwell shows how grotesque pleasure
can be found by training a black of meager intelligence to
perform tricks which ought to bring embarrassment to both
trainer and audience. The attitude of both could only be
that the black had the status of an animal. The story goes
that after New Year's dinner a servant is sent for Blue Boy.
His opening act is to give an unintelligible account of how he
bit a shoat to death. Then he is caused to drop to the floor
and go through eccentric motions which amused the guests
but which left him exhausted. In a period of five years,
dating from when the landowner noticed him at the age of
twelve, Blue Boy had been trained, obeying all commands
to perform tricks to please his owner and friends. Sending
him to an institution, it is explained, would result in avoiding much enjoyment. On demand, he shuffled his feet so
violently the arteries in his head swelled visibly. Extreme,
weird, physical manifestations were prized by the plantation
owner. His gruesome tricks were important enough even
to eliminate the need for his working in the field or doing
other chores. Not only did the whites display an absence
of "human feeling, " but also they evidently forgot, and had
to forget, the people they were using were human.

Say: Is This the U.S.A. ? (1941), dedicated quite
properly to Erskine's father, has a number of suggestions
about racial degradation. It contains, too, this anecdote:
between Omaha and Kansas City, at midnight, about an hour
from its destination, a train the Caldwells were on stopped.
A black youth, about sixteen, a sweater wrapped about his
head and another wrapped around his chest, got on and went
to sleep as soon as he was seated. Shortly after, the conductor, upon finding the boy did not have the fare, stopped
the train and prepared to eject him. One offer to lend the
passenger his fare was rejected by the conductor. When the
conductor was told he would have to take the fare if it was
offered, he said that was not true in the case of a black and
put him off.

A different manifestation of anti-black feeling is found
in "The Negro in the Well." Jule Robinson finds that Bokus
Bradley, a black, has fallen into his well. Before he will
do anything to help the unfortunate neighbor out of his
predicament, Robinson forces him to agree to an outrageous-
ly unfair trade so as to get some hunting dogs belonging to
Bradley that Robinson had coveted. One would think a white
would not have tried to convince another white that such a
trade was necessary as the price of what should be considered the most normal of assistance. Or, any white who had
been gouged in such a way would not have felt any need to
stick to his bargain--indeed, social pressure could be brought
against any one who would try such a stunt. But Caldwell's
observation is that the black is convinced that, things being
what they were/are, the white could get away with it.

Ego bruises such as that had a compound effect leading to a brutal view of life. Two episodes in "Inspiration
for Greatness" (ca. 1930) suggest the way the life of the
black is conditioned by a lack of what a white would consider normal consideration. A sawmill hand had his foot
crushed under a huge log. Instead of seeing to proper
medical attention, the mill foreman cuts the smashed member off. The black takes the foot, wrapped in newspaper,
home with him. Such a necessarily toughened response to
the circumstances of life is also demonstrated in relationships between blacks. In another section of "Inspiration
for Greatness," a black is shot to death. Two other blacks
quarrel over his knife. One antagonist tears out the other
man's tongue and throws it into the river. In "Savannah
River Pay Day" the gold teeth are knocked out of the mouth
of a black worker who has accidentally been killed.

Not only are the blacks thought to be insensitive--
or made to be--but they are also thought to be stupid.
Jim Leslie, in God's Little Acre, thinks the talk about the
special powers of an albino is the sort of thing one would
hear from blacks and that a white ought not to fall for such
superstition. In Search of Bisco records the remark that
the reason for segregated schools is that black brains are
not yet big enough to compete with white. Another person
remarks in that book that perhaps in a few more generations
blacks might know enough to vote. White is generally
assumed to be better. Some even say it. The characters
in Journeyman (1935) say as a matter of routine things like,
"If you decide to do things like white folks...." Or a sense

of identity is suggested by saying, "We're all white here."
In You Have Seen Their Faces it is casually noted, in a
caption showing a room full of black children in a classroom
in Scotts, Arkansas, that the story they are listening to involves white girls who are transformed into princesses.

A central episode of In Search of Bisco involves
Caldwell's being in mid-Georgia when he was nearly six--
thus in the summer of 1908. His playmate is Bisco, the
latter-day search for whom gives the book its title, son
of black parents who live nearby. A day of play ends with
his going home with Bisco, eating with him, and getting
ready to crawl into bed with him. But Bisco's mother,
realizing the relationship is getting to a stage where it is
going to create problems, dresses him and delivers him to
his parents. His mother insists to him the importance
of his promising never to go to Bisco's house again. The
significance of this account is intensified by the realization
that, in the summer of 1908, the Caldwells no longer lived
in Georgia but rather in Prosperity, S. C. It is also somewhat against what we know of the personality of his father
and mother, though Erskine says she was more conservative
than his father, to think that there would be parental insistence on segregation. Some of the episode is imaginary;
perhaps all of it is. But his making it up shows how important a point it was in the lives of many children. Sooner
or later they were taught about the dividing line. He told
a black friend in 1965 that he had never differentiated people
on the basis of race, and that is doubtless an accurate statement of his life and his ambition for others as shown throughout his work.

As a counterpoint to the learned difference factor
just mentioned is the remark quoted elsewhere in the same
book: It is natural for blacks and whites to be segregated.
In considering this, it is mentioned that whites think there
are sanitary reasons for not eating out of the same dishes
and not sleeping in the same bed with some one from a
different race. Then it is mentioned that it seems to be
all right for blacks to prepare food for whites and nurse
white babies. In Journeyman, the little white boy, Vearl,
plays all day with the cabin children. He lives in the
cabin. But he does not sleep with the black children. He
sleeps in a bed with two black adults. Associating with
blacks will be accepted as a necessity, of course. Gene
Morgan, in The Bastard, is abandoned by his degenerate

mother. An old black woman offers to raise the baby and
saves him from his mother, who wants to solve her problem
by killing him. She raises him till he is eleven, at which
time he runs away. He, reacting as a typical white, likes
the blacks of whom he can make use.

As late as 1963 (in Around About America), Caldwell
was noting that a kind of lowest common denominator of
racial suppression in the South is the fact that both water
and liquor must be obtained through separate facilities by
a black. The Earnshaw Neighborhood (1971) mentions a
separate graveyard for blacks. In Search of Bisco (1965)
records the bizarre solution to the burial problem used by
one black. Because he could not afford a burial plot for
his father, because there was no free burial ground for
blacks, as there was for whites, and because the body had
to be buried by a certain time, he buried the body in a
hole dug in a bank of earth overlooking a state highway. A
rusty advertising sign for a bread company marked the spot.

In You Have Seen Their Faces Caldwell says that a
fault of the South is that the whites have neither integrated
with blacks nor tolerated them. In Search of Bisco points
out that pay is better in the North but that life there is
segregated, too. He seems to feel that the reputation for
courtesy and hospitality of the South, however, make the
violence and stubbornness of the tradition of racial suppression and separation more striking. The root of the tradition
is a combined sense of guilt and insecurity. The black is
dedicatedly characterized as inadequate and dangerous in
order to justify white attacks that really are aimed at
quieting their sense of fear. Whites' fear is based on the
realization, conscious or unconscious, of present and past
injustice. Like Troy Pickett in Summertime Island (1968),
the whites think the blacks should do just what the whites
want them to--which, it will be recalled, is to produce as
much as possible for the smallest possible reward. Knowing
fully well they could never put up with such an arrangement
themselves, whites naturally fear all approaches to equal
status for blacks. The prospect of being paid back in their
own coin creates a very substantial fear. The whites have
no intention of being discriminated against in the way the
blacks have. And they can easily believe the blacks would
want to even the score after all they have been through.

The bane of Troy Pickett's existence, the black

teacher, Duke, wants only to progress normally in society. He senses especially the way he is restrained from moving freely about the country. Unhappily, there are whites for whom the bottom will drop out of everything if they can not depend on having the blacks below them in the social order. Sister Bessie, in Tobacco Road, so needy a person in terms of acceptance that she has made up a religion of one, hopes when she passes the blacks in her new car that they will know it belongs to her. Such people need to think that any mysterious sound is caused by stealthy blacks (A Home in the Uplands). Troy expresses his disappointment at owing any kind of debt of gratitude to a black; in this case it is because he was saved from drowning by Duke. He is also disgusted when other whites do not express hatred of blacks. He thinks city people do not understand the menace of blacks, who multiply rapidly and threaten to take control if not intimidated and restrained. When a black man is given a drink of liquor and a white juvenile is not, he takes this to be a case of favoritism. There is a constant suggestion of paranoia in the situation, manifested in every conceivable way.

No reasonable pattern can be expected to emerge in the tortured emotional climate of white consideration of the blacks. At the same time they are expressing the fear that blacks will conspire to overwhelm them, whites contend that the blacks can be manipulated through a system of rewards and punishments (In Search of Bisco). Additionally, Caldwell has found that the whites think the government in Washington has caused the discontent which has made the blacks want equal treatment. A middle-of-the-road white southerner, also recorded in In Search of Bisco, thought that television shows which featured blacks perverted the ideas of southern blacks.

A further exemplification of the insane pressure to triumph over the black at any cost is seen when Troy excuses his ingratitude to Duke for saving his life by saying that Duke only did it so he could boast about it. Troy recalls that, even in childhood, he hit black children with fist, bottle, and rock and left boards with projecting nails so that bare black feet might encounter them in the grass. As an adult, he harasses black pedestrians with his truck, making them jump out of the way and hoping to hit them. Even though Troy places much dependence on having his whiteness recognized, he beats up a store owner who insults

Duke. His damaged ego will try to find reassurance in
victory over anyone, including teenage black girls. The
blacks, under the system in the South, are those most vul-
nerable to sick people such as Troy.

In the insecure atmosphere which creates segregation,
strange fetishes may be expected. A white prostitute in
Poor Fool will let a black customer do anything he wants but
excepts kissing. After Troy has defended black Duke against
the insult of the shopkeeper, he asks Duke to bend over so
he can kick him lightly. He accompanies the token hostility
with a reminder that blacks and whites are totally separated.
Troy is visiting a violent revenge on innocent people for a
grudge he is not even aware of. The same is true of Clyde
in Close to Home: he was originally a wrestler but was
barred from the ring for killing an opponent. As a deputy
sheriff he finds an approved outlet for his frustrated life in
riding herd on blacks.

Erskine's father, the Rev. I. S. Caldwell, was
greatly interested in crime and punishment. He wrote in
one of his columns in an Augusta newspaper, "We never
learn how to deal with the criminals we create." He attacked the chain gangs, the main instrument of punishment
of real and supposed crimes by blacks (and, to a consid-
erably lesser extent, by whites) in Georgia, of which his
son later wrote, and other southern states. Erskine had
spent his Sundays in Wrens getting to know the blacks on
the chain gangs instead of going to church; he included pictures of the gangs in You Have Seen Their Faces (1937).
When he and Margaret Bourke-White approached one gang in
their automobile, the guard fired at them. Erskine was
able to get written permission for pictures and then had to
read the document to the illiterate man in charge.

The chain gang fit well the disposition in the South
to resist equal rights with perseverance, imagination and
brutality. The enforcement of civil rights laws is limited,
In Search of Bisco says, because the whites in power do
not want them enforced. That book depicts the attitude of
a town as white, regardless of what the law says. People
who have that point of view also think that certain actions
have to be taken to let blacks know they mean to maintain
control (Deep South). In Place Called Estherville, people
of the town boasted of being hard on blacks and gave that
as the reason for the lack of racial problems, by which

they meant that the desired climate of black obedience was maintained. In such a situation the job of the police is not to serve justice equally but rather to maintain unequal pressures. In The Weather Shelter (1969), Caldwell shows a situation in which the police actively harass a white man who has his brown son in the car. The car is carefully watched all the time it is in town; overnight, they record its movements. The next morning they question the driver as to how long he is staying and tell him that the two ate in the wrong place, that they wrongly visited the black section of town, and that the boy (being brown and thus black) should be sitting in the back of the car.

In discussion of court treatment of a black offender in The Weather Shelter, Caldwell makes it clear that he does not believe proper judicial procedures are used. Willie Shoelong, a black barber from Memphis, speeds through Wolverton. The police have to force his car off the road. He comes out of it with a knife in his hand. He is subdued and jailed. Before his trial, the comment is that he will get a year at hard labor and not just a speeding fine. The police and the judge have already determined that matter.

Caldwell had had his own experience with perversion of justice when, at the age of 19, he was jailed in Bogalusa, Louisiana. The incident had such an impact that he used it as the basis for two different accounts, one in Call It Experience and the other in Deep South. He owed his landlady rent because the manager of a magazine crew ran off with the money he was to have received. The woman sent him after a non-existent job and arranged for him to be picked up by the police. The arrest sheet says he "did maliciously and wilfully loiter around suspicious places without being able to give a satisfactory reason therefor." It took him some days to smuggle a message to his father in Georgia to make arrangements for him to be able to pay the money to get released. Certainly the vague and inclusive charges made against him would help him to sympathize with the blacks of In Search of Bisco, who said they were arrested by biased police for bumping some one accidentally on the sidewalk. (They were doubtless maliciously loitering, too....)

On the trips made collecting information for In Search of Bisco, Caldwell was so aware of the zealous watch of police for people making observations relating to the treat-

ment of blacks that he drove rented cars. As he went
from one state to another, he stopped in the office of the
rental agency and had the license changed. He did not feel
a car with out-of-state plates was safe in the South (in 1965).
Naturally, it has been only with reluctance that whites have
allowed blacks to participate in government. Handsome
Brown, who was expected to do any work which properly
fell to the lot of Morris Stroup, had absolutely no relationship to Stroup's brief tenure as Collector of Waifs and
Strays. And that was probably quite acceptable to him.
He had learned that any contact with the law was more
likely to be unpleasant than not. Thus, when the town
marshal approaches the Stroup household to collect a family
member who is an escaped convict, Handsome, without knowing anything about it, gets off the woodpile where he had
been sitting and goes into the barn.

Duke, the black school teacher in Summertime Island,
recalls having been harassed by policemen while window-
shopping in town and told to go back to the black area. He
recalls telling the police that he was a teacher, only to be
accused of boasting. One officer was not content to make
him leave but insisted he run or be put in jail. Duke says
it is the same all over and not improving. Blacks pictured
in jail in such places as Saluda, S. C. , in Say: Is This the
U. S. A. ?, suggest their offenses were either nonexistent or
minor and that the officers do not seem to be able to get
white offenders into jail. In Close to Home, though she is
"guilty" only of miscegenation, for which no charge will be
filed, a sheriff is told to charge a mulatto, Josene, with
something. It is routine to charge black girls with prostitution. It is an easy way to deal with them, for they can
not afford legal costs of any kind. The woman who presses
charges, because her husband is in love with the black girl,
accepts this as a way to put Josene in jail for six months.

The same woman makes, in the course of her efforts
to get her husband and Josene jailed for miscegenation, a
visit to the jail. She demands that the black prisoners stop
singing. She is bothered by the fact that people are in the
jail and wants to know what they did. The jailer casually
explains they have done mostly nothing and will soon be out
again. When the woman leaves, the jailer asks the black
prisoners to start singing again, for he rather likes the
entertainment.

Both Ganus and Kathyanne, the main characters of

Place Called Estherville (1949), are used to show how harassment could be expected to occur in a way having only the
most tenuous of relationships with the official structure of
society. Ganus is menaced and insulted in an alley by a
group of boys ten to sixteen years of age. It starts with
him being hit on the head with a thrown rock. He is criticized for complaining about being hit. He suffers various
other indignities and is made to take off his trousers and
threatened with emasculation, the operation being mentioned
as being beneficial to a black. Several of the boys, who
have been spurned by a contemporary living in the same
house where Ganus works, are particularly virulent and
jealous in their suggestions as to what should be done to
Ganus, venting sexual frustration on their hapless captive.
In this tense atmosphere, he is asked to say whether he
thinks white or black girls are better. The author inter-
polates a reference to a similar problem put to a black
preacher: Is Christ black or white?

        The situation is given some relief by the accidental
appearance of a townsman, who, incredibly, accepts Ganus'
enforced assurance that everything is all right. After the
man leaves, the momentum of the episode is broken. A
boy whose father is known for beating blacks with a club
contents himself with cutting a gash in Ganus' shoulder.
As they leave, one boy tells Ganus he did not mean a thing
he said. Another threatens him with harm if he complains
to any one. As he separates himself from the group, a
rock falls behind him.

        Kathyanne is abducted by a group of teenagers, for
one of whose mothers she works, as she passes a drugstore
at night. The boys manage to escape detection and smuggle
her into a small building. They contemplate her animalis-
tically, insisting to her that a black girl will not tell of
anything that happens; only a white girl would do that. After
she is roughly menaced, she takes off her clothes. One of
the boys knows that his father took a black girl off the
streets and kept her in his store half the night. He had to
buy his wife a fur coat as an indemnity. A smaller boy,
scared, turns to Kathyanne for protection. She puts her
arm around him but says nothing. The scene is interrupted
by the town marshal. He disperses the boys and tells them
to stay outside the town limits when engaging in such activities. The officer, though he knows better, professes to
believe that she was illegally displaying herself. He knows

she can not get up in court and testify effectively against
five white boys. She will be fined $25, he tells her, but
says perhaps he can find some one to pay the fine. He
offers to do it himself, but she refuses him. In his anger
at her rejection, he strikes her. She tells him that some
day he will pay for his mistreatment of people. Smarting
from what was actually a sexual refusal, he says that blacks
are stupid to prefer their own kind. The big trouble with
blacks, he tells her, is that they learn so slowly. Kathyanne replies she will be pleased when she eventually hears
that he has been shot. He hustles her to the jail.

        As Erskine Caldwell was to write in an article for
the New Masses of January 30, 1934, the need for justice
for blacks was (and certainly still seems to be) like a
boiling kettle which would blow its lid off. The general
climate of pseudo-law which gives a basis for that idea
has already been described. A more formal catalogue of
unpunished offenses against blacks will now be presented
from his works. The episode involving Kathyanne and the
teenagers was, of course, a matter of the crime of abduction. It will be noticed that the marshal, focused on his
own particular brand of wrong-doing, does not even remark
it. The inadequate sheriff of Trouble in July, after one of
his prisoners has been taken as a replacement in case the
intended victim of a lynching is not apprehended, does
assert that it is an offense to abduct any one, even blacks.
The Ku Klux Klan is mentioned in This Very Earth (1948)
as running a black out of the state. This may or may not
have involved abduction. But there is no doubt about a seg-
ment of "Hours Before Eternity" (ca. 1930): the narrator
says a black girl that he was sent for would not come.
The abductor tells him to follow with a harnessed mule.
He backs the mule into place and hooks it up to the chain
while the abductor, having knocked the girl unconscious,
wraps it around her body. The mule having been kicked
into activity, drags the girl on the ground to the house of
her captor. The chain is forged tight around her and
spiked to the floor.

        A very moving section of Deep South (1968) deals
with arson committed against the True Life Fellowship
church. A complaint was filed with the police about disturbance to neighbors from music and singing on Sunday
evenings. The minister, Rumson Tatum, a black handyman
in a town where the Rev. Ira S. Caldwell had a church, is

told that his church will be closed if there is any more
difficulty. An effort was made, in the summer weather, to
have the services with windows and shutters closed. In
response to the extreme heat, the sound did eventually
burst forth. A little after midnight the building was on
fire. There was little water available in the black section,
but what there was the firemen used to wet down adjacent
houses. Forty years later, because it was being used for
meetings of people who were picketing to be allowed service
at a nearby truck stop, Rumson Tatum's second church was
set aflame. Additionally, the picketers were advised by the
police that continued activity would lead to more fires.

　　　Assault on the person of blacks can be exemplified
over and over. A black whose mule stepped in a rabbit
hole and became lame was beaten into unconsciousness,
his boss knowing he would be afraid to defend himself. The
owner in A House in the Uplands beats blacks with a chain.
Ganus, in Place Called Estherville, is befriended by a white
housewife. Her husband is angry about that and strikes
Ganus across the chest with a heavy piece of wood. As
Ganus leaves, he is struck again in the back of the head.
In the same book, the fact that blacks are beaten when they
do not display appropriate attitudes and when they are found
in places deemed inappropriate is given as the reason for
the low incidence of "racial trouble." The deputy sheriff
in Close to Home always makes it a point to knock blacks
down before taking them to jail.

　　　In The Bastard one is introduced to two black teenage girls who have already become prostitutes. Their price
is a quarter. After Gene has flipped a coin to see which
one will be patronized, the other one leaves. A chapter in
This Very Earth (1948) is devoted to the forcing of two
black girls to participate in sexual initiation of a white boy.
Chism Crockett takes his son with him when he herds the
two girls into a freight car, against their urgent pleas.
They were on their way home from work. After they realize what is inevitable, the girls object futilely to the presence
of the boy and the fact that one of them is married. Among
other threats is reference to the Ku Klux Klan. By the use
of threats that evoke unpleasantness they evidently know very
well, the girls are forced to surrender, thus providing a
telling lesson in sex and race relationships for the son.

　　　One of Caldwell's most vivid stories, "The People vs.

Abe Lathan, Colored, " is used to give the key to the whole
upside-down legal system endured by the blacks. He is one
of those used-up farm laborers, having worked on the same
place for forty years. The owner wants to evict him. He
feels he has earned his place. For complaining about being
evicted, he is charged with threatening to do bodily harm
and arrested as well as evicted. In contrast to the lack of
concern of the owner, even the deputy which carries through
the legal action feels sorry for Lathan. As will be seen
later, he has no legal recourse and is headed for the chain
gang. As has been suggested elsewhere, a black might
expect some form of false arrest for any show of spirit or
awkwardness.

Erskine's own consciousness of this physical abuse
of blacks was intensified by the fact that his father had a
haunting memory of a flogging of a convict. In Some American People it is noted that whippings were among those
means used to repress requests for better land or equipment
or for fair recompense. A passage in You Have Seen Their
Faces speculates that perhaps there were only a few ten-
foot whips striking the backs of sharecroppers at the time
it was written (1937). But it was certain in Caldwell's
mind that any white man who felt he wanted to or needed
to beat or whip or maul a black could do so. Physical in-
timidation had taken the place of legal slavery. The blacks
had been bred to fuse in their minds the idea of obedience
to God and their masters. Generally, they knew the rules
after many decades of suppression, and followed them. The
pain of their bodies supplied any needed reminder.

The matter of innumerable frauds perpetrated on the
blacks by whites at all levels can not be ignored either.
Because the purpose of having blacks in the country in the
first place was to exploit them, taking further advantage of
them by dishonest practices and misrepresentations was,
then, considered natural and allowable. A first aspect of
the procedure was to encourage and insure illiteracy--that
would stop the blacks from knowing any better than they were
told. As explained in A House in the Uplands (1946), the
system had always been to keep the blacks perpetually in
fear and in debt and thus to get them to work for nothing
or as close to it as possible. Imaginary debts, virtually
unchallengeable by illiterates, were consistently resorted to.

At the other end of the scale of injustice to blacks

was the community inflammation called lynching. Doubtless
Caldwell had heard all his life the kind of incident recorded
in his father's column of January 16, 1931, under the title,
"Civilization Is Only Skin Deep. " The elder Caldwell refers
to a case in which a black who had killed a teacher was
tied to the roof of a schoolroom: "After the building was
saturated with gasoline, a match was struck and the savage
that is in men made several thousand people watch the
cringing, screaming man as his blood was licked up by the
raging fire.   A generation is not sufficient to erase the
degrading effects of lynching. " Before that was written,
Caldwell had already written a poem about lynching, either
at the University of Virginia or in his early days in Maine.
(One of the two manuscript copies of the poem has the Mount
Vernon address in the upper right hand corner.) The device
of the poem is that the lynched body, hanging from a shot-
torn tree, can speak to the writer.   The body tells how his
killers had fought over the ears and hands they had taken
as souvenirs.   The writer records the fact that he clasped
the arm of the black body, guarded by weeping trees.

        Though he is quoted at least once in such a way as
to allow the inference that he had witnessed a lynching,
Caldwell's response to a direct question was that he several
times got to the scene of a lynching before the body was
removed but had never been in attendance, as, presumably,
he would not have wanted to be.   In Tennessee (from 1915
to 1919) and Georgia (1919 to 1920) he tried to get to the
scene as quickly as possible when rumors that an event
was impending or that the hunt was on.   Perhaps even he
could not say whether he actually wanted to see one take
place.

Caldwell's first specific memory of lynching, as discussed
in In Search of Bisco, dates from September, 1917, when
he was fourteen and living in Atoka, Tennessee, near
Memphis, where his father was minister of the Salem
A. R. P. Church.   He describes how he heard that a black
youth, a laborer in a saw mill, had been accused of raping
a white girl and had been hanged in a tree and his body
shredded with gunfire.   School friends said the girl was
known to ask for candy and then undress, pleading to be
embraced.   He had heard men say that the girl had lied
and that "Sonny" should not have been executed.   Others

thought any black man who had sex with a white woman, even a prostitute, should be killed.

While he was at the University of Virginia, Caldwell began to write about the lynchings which were an all-too-common part of the social scene he was assessing. His first published article, written while he was in Charlottes-ville in 1926, refers to what he called "one of the most disgusting cases of mob violence in the history" of Georgia. An insane black patient in the asylum in Milledgeville had attacked and killed his white, female nurse with a pick handle. A small gang of men took him out into Wilkinson County, secured him to a tree, and bludgeoned him to death, also with a pick handle. Caldwell points out that no legal action has been taken nor may be expected. He states that very few will regret the brutality to an insane person.

His classic stories, "Kneel to the Rising Sun" and "Saturday Afternoon," were published in the Thirties. The first deals with the killing of a black who dares to protest his mistreatment. His friend is forced to betray him to those who are hunting him. "Saturday Afternoon" in quiet desperation focuses on the callous pleasure with which the men of a small town welcome the influx into the deadness of afternoon of the excitement of a lynching. Soft drinks are sold at the site of the execution.

In the unpublished novelette, If Only to Remember the Flat-Lands, written in 1930 while he was living in Portland, Maine, Caldwell used lynching strategically to set the tone of a small Georgia town, based on Wrens, where he had lived in 1919 and 1920. His main character is a youth who is about to go to college, as Erskine had been. Donald is anxious to score a big scoop for the nearby city paper. Over-eager, he hears a man exclaim that he is going to lynch a certain black man. The youth writes a story of what he assumes will take place and gives it to the tele-grapher at the railroad station for transmission. In addi-tion to the evident commonness of referring to such actions and the assumption of the threatened event, the fact that the boy has no regret or concern about the matter, is interested in it only as an exciting news event, doubtless reveals what Caldwell considers the state of social consciousness in the town at that time.

In articles in the January 16 and January 23, 1934,

New Masses, Erskine Caldwell reported on three lynchings
in and around Barton, Georgia, in the vicinity of Wrens.
One black was shot on the street in Barton; another was
beaten with short pieces of pipe and his body thrown in the
well.   The third had six bullets fired into his head and chest
and then was nearly decapitated before his body was left in
a field.   A coroner's jury had found that the killers of all
three were "parties unknown. "   Two weeks before a black
had been shot by two white men while he lay in bed.   The
men who did the deed admitted it, explaining to the jury
that they went to the wrong house.   After they were acquitted,
they promised to get the right black the next time.

    Caldwell reports that it is anyone's guess how many
lynchings have occurred in the vicinity of Barton in the pre-
ceding years.   A white farmer guessed that it might have
been as many as twenty.   A black stated that only the devil
knows.   It is pointed out that none of the four weekly papers
in the county have mentioned the lynchings in question.
Caldwell says the rule seems to be: "If a white man is
murdered, telegraph it in; if a Negro is murdered, mail it
in. "   The New Masses reported on February 6 that Caldwell's personal safety had been threatened because of the
reports he had sent in on the lynchings.   Both Erskine and
his father were reported as willing to testify before a grand
jury about how the killers were triumphantly walking the
streets.   The Solicitor-General of Georgia is quoted as saying the killings the Caldwells were complaining about were
not extraordinary.

    Thus by 1935, when an exhibition of An Art Com-
mentary on Lynching was held in the Norton Galleries in
New York, Erskine Caldwell was sufficiently well known for
his opposition to the crime that he was asked to prepare
"A Note, " a one-page statement, which accompanied the
catalogue for the showing.   Reviewing the circumstances of
lynching, he calls for anti-lynching laws as necessary to
promote the lifting of the cultural standards of the white
population so as to eliminate the practice, which degrades
all concerned.   Not only does the illegal killing of blacks--
and the threat of it--repress the one race, Caldwell pointed
out, but also such sadistic indulgence in killing and torture
degrades those who participate and those who live in the
community where it happens.   Seventy-five years of it,
dating from the outbreak of the Civil War, have proved,
Caldwell's "Note" continued, that action from outside the

group of southern states, which was almost always the scene
of this particular crime, would be necessary.

     When Margaret Bourke-White and Erskine Caldwell
did their photo-essay on the South, You Have Seen Their
Faces, in 1936 and 1937, they were particularly interested
in the status of blacks--forty of their seventy-one pictures
were of blacks. Their trail took them into knowledge of a
lynching-in-progress at Kelley, Georgia. The elements of
the case were these: (1) the black who reportedly raped
a white girl had a "bad" reputation; (2) the girl was generally known as a prostitute; (3) but she was white; (4) and
he was black; (5) the race was on between the mob and
the sheriff; (6) the man would be lynched if the mob got
there first. In a letter of July 21, 1936, Margaret wrote
that they saw the beginnings of the lynching but that the
sheriff got there first.

     Caldwell's fullest treatment of the subject appears in
his book, Trouble in July, published in 1940. Sonny Clark,
an eighteen-year-old field hand who has only been to the
county seat a few times and whose main interest in life is
his pet rabbits, is accosted by the nymphomaniac daughter
of an emotionally-deprived white sharecropper. The girl's
false accusation is supported by a middle-aged Bible mer-
chant, who resents the appearance of a competitive black
Bible. The girl, after seeing Sonny's bullet-torn body hanging in a tree, hysterically proclaims his innocence. The
residual crowd at the scene shift their hostility and stone
her to death. Readers will notice a distressed puzzlement
on the part of Caldwell over all sorts of violence, which he
records in many connections. The stoning of the girl is
reminiscent of many other scenes in which the thirst for
violence seems difficult to quench. He records in The
Sacrilege of Alan Kent, written about 1930, that, after a
lynching, as the men anticipate going home, they wanted
souvenirs. Digits of the hands and feet were cut off and
put in pockets. An attempt to take the arms was abandoned
because of difficulty in separation from the body.

     To this extremely grim matter, Caldwell brings, in
the person of the sheriff, a sad humor. Naturally, a
society that was not serious about the enforcement of its
laws would have incapable police officers. Caldwell gives
a full portrait of such criminal ineptitude in Trouble in July.
It has long been the sheriff's habit to go fishing, which he

hates, when a lynching is in progress.   He knows he will
not remain in office if he does his duty.   As matters develop, the judge, who is the political boss of the county,
tells him he had better get out in the county and pretend
to try to capture the fugitive.   The sheriff tries to disasso-
ciate himself from the matter by locking himself in the jail,
planning to claim he was overpowered and placed there.
He notes with pleasure that another inmate is Sam, a black
who keeps running afoul of the legal requirements concerning mortgages on used cars.   The lynchers arrive at the
jail and take the second innocent black as a hostage.   They
plan to kill him if Sonny escapes.

    This aspect of the case causes the sheriff to spend
time stumbling around the countryside looking for Sam, for
whom he has a genuine, but ineffectual, regard.   He does
not, of course, forget to stop and do some vote-seeking on
the way.   He is an indolent beleaguered slob who feels a
vague sympathy for the innocent victim but also feels violently threatened by the high-tension potential of the situation.   He is physically hampered by his fatness and his
constant need for food and sleep.   The sheriff rightly thinks
that he will find only trouble in attempting to deal with the
lynchers, who are drunk, determined--even desperate--and
full of energy.   They do not want any interference with
their horrible fun.   The group is highly reminiscent of a
gang in The Weather Shelter (published in 1969).

    The father of the girl who was supposedly raped does
not believe anything happened to her, for he knows her.
But he does not want anything to ruin the prospect of dragging
the culprit through the county behind his car before turning
him over for execution.   Officially the outraged father of a
violated daughter, he says he would just as soon shoot the
sheriff as a rapist and is bitterly disappointed when someone
else finds Sonny first.   He is a sharecropper, like those in
You Have Seen Their Faces who, having been replaced by
blacks, will walk six miles to a lynching, looking for release of their resentment and desperation.   They press their
quarry with the same vicious fervor of a 'possum hunt.   (A
deputy sheriff in Trouble in July, used to hunting, says he
enjoys tracking blacks whenever the occasion allows.)
During their search for Sonny, the men surge into the black
quarter of the farm where he lives.   Balked of their prey,
they beat a black man with a barrel stave, pour turpentine
on his wife's genitals, gang-rape a black girl, and set fire
to a chicken house.

In contrast with the excited and extreme acts of the
pursuers, Caldwell depicts a bewildered and passive prey.
Sonny, whose parents had been killed in an accident, lives
with and supports his grandmother. Bewildered as he is by
the sudden complication of his life, events which he really
does not comprehend, he moves with agonizing deliberateness
in preparing to escape, something he is completely unfitted
for. He terrifies the other cabin-dwellers by appearing and
saying he has been accosted on the road by a white girl.
The blacks instantly tell him to leave and go as far north
as possible as rapidly as possible. He stubbornly insists
that he had no chance to dissuade or evade the girl.

Sonny's friend, who knows blacks will not be allowed
to interfere, ejects him from his cabin, having told him
what to do. Sonny clings to the steps. He is still there
some time later, seemingly almost paralyzed, saying he does
not know where to go. His departure is excruciating. He
decides he can hide out in the woods. Then he returns to
his friend's cabin to say he is hungry. His friend tells
him the dead do not need food. After being slipped some
cornbread through the door, he finally starts across the
fields. Then he thinks of his rabbits and decides he had
better feed them before he goes. He momentarily forgets
his impending doom in the pleasure he finds in his pets.
When he does, at length, leave, he has a rabbit buttoned
inside his shirt.

Although the county is boiling with people looking
for him, he is not captured by any of them, presumably
because his actions are so completely free of guilty motiva-
tion. The man who accidentally discovers him in a weed
patch is torn between turning him in or not. After the
lynching, which he properly assumes will occur, he knows he
will hate the fact. Sonny seals his fate by pleading to be
hidden. The man knows he cannot afford the guilty association of actively aiding the fugitive. Sonny docilely follows
his captor, who does not even have a gun. The farmer,
after he has heard Sonny's story, is convinced that he does
not deserve punishment, but he thinks he must turn him in.
On learning this, Sonny asks to be shot. The farmer refuses on the grounds that he does not have a gun.

Sonny's captor feels not the first stirrings of re-
morse, sympathy, or concern. The suggestion is that
black Sonny, like any other animal in distress, might have

to be put out of his misery by means of a bullet.   There is
a small group of other people who think the sheriff should
gain custody of and guard a suspect until a trial is held.
It is noted that they hold it against him for going fishing
during the last lynching.   This small group is apparently
ineffectual, though the sheriff hates to lose their votes.   It
is, of course, impossible to please everybody.   A woman
calls the jail to say she is afraid that her husband, who
is out hunting for Sonny, will be hurt.   She is also afraid
for her own safety.

When the owner of the plantation on which Sonny
lived and worked calls, the sheriff thinks it is just another
fool who wanted the lynching prevented.   But the farmer is
the practical type who does not want to lose a good hand.
Nor does he want a mob racing through his fields, damaging
crops.   He knows, too, that the lynching will suppress the
activity of other blacks, who are needed to get in the harvest.
He cows the hands who come to the farm, shooting behind
them as they leave, muttering that the sheriff would not have
interfered.

A bizarre sub-plot in Trouble in July is the petition
for Congress to provide for sending all blacks back to Africa
that is circulated by a widow who sells bibles.   She is in-
furiated to find that the blacks have been buying Black Jesus
bibles by mail from Chicago.   That interferes with her live-
lihood.   When she discusses her proposed solution of sending
the blacks to Africa with a U. S. senator, he tells her he
will act in the matter if she can persuade everyone in Georgia
to sign a petition in favor of that procedure.

Though she was a witness to the encounter on the
basis of which the girl has falsely accused Sonny of molesting
her, she realizes that the furor attendant on a lynching will
help her cause.   Though she was raised among blacks and
always "treated them right," the materialistic considerations
of the threat of the Black Bible make her forget her morality.
She feels, rightly, that either a lynching or the lack of it
could make people sign her petition as an instrument of their
resentment.   The judge who is the political boss of the county
agrees that people might sign the foolish document at random
and tears it up.   The sheriff points out that many of the
people it is proposed to send back to Africa were born in
their county.   The idea which deals a death blow to the petition is that the blacks are needed to do the work.   No one

wanted to consider further a future in which the blacks were
not there to handle the hard labor.   An occasional lynching
to keep them in line (and provide that special violent entertainment) was much preferable.

The cornerstone of the whole structure of the reversal
of justice or the negation of it where the blacks were/are
concerned is simple failure to do the assigned job.   The
sheriff of the county in Trouble in July is an outstanding
example.   Readers will find he has neither freedom nor intention nor capability to serve the law as he should.   All
he knows is that he wants to get elected again the next
time.   And he knows that the voters do not want him to
serve the interests of justice when it comes to blacks.   The
events of the novel show how the lynchers make meaningful
their insistence to him that he stay out of the matter.   A
lynching could not take place if there were alert and determined law enforcement.   Caldwell suggests that a sheriff
who insisted on having no lynchings would not remain in
office and might not remain uninjured.   Nonetheless, in the
last few lines of the book Caldwell makes it certain that he
is calling attention to the failure of the sheriff to do his job,
as his oath of office says, "without fear or favor."   He has
shown favor and has been almost completely lacking in
courage.   He reckons, in the last speech of the book, that
he had "sort of forgotten" about that part of the oath.

The inaction of the officials willed by the electorate
made possible the lynchings which have already been mentioned.   And they affirmed the general practice of the murder
of blacks, which many whites thought essential to their effective repression.   A character in Journeyman says he does
not mind seeing a dead black now and then.   After the sawmill incident in The Bastard, the owner says no one says
anything about the fact that a black gets split open (or sawed
up) periodically.   In Search of Bisco (1965) contains the
statement that whites in Mississippi kill blacks readily and
without penalty.   Bodies are thrown into wells with no consequences.   Nightriders can make blacks disappear.   Cement
may be stuffed into the body, or it may be weighted down
with iron before being thrown into a swamp.   "Hours Before Eternity" has a situation in which a black reported
himself to be too ill to do his work.   He was shot and in-
terred in a dung heap.   "Indian Summer" tells of an episode
involving how white boys at play give a near-fatal ducking
to a black boy.

Caldwell depicts the casual attitude of law enforcement officers toward homicide in The Last Night of Summer
(1963). A radio report during the night mentions three
murders, one of a black in a pool room, and predicts one
more before morning. Police officers who find their work
an outlet for their hatred of blacks are not unknown. They
know that the general populace will support them in their
practice of killing troublesome blacks. In both Close to
Home and The Weather Shelter police officers shoot blacks
needlessly and claim self defense. The one in Close to
Home makes it a point to knock down any black he arrests,
has killed several blacks, always pleaded self-defense, and
has never even been charged, let alone whitewashed. It is
in "Candy-Man Beechum" that Caldwell gives this theme of
gratuitous and unpunished killing its most powerful treatment. Candy-Man is just an exuberant black, going his
way, enjoying life. In full stride, he meets the cold restraint of the paranoid law officer who cuts him down in
the street. Caldwell commented that writing a story like
that meant more to him than creating a hundred pages.

The sheriff's deputy in Close to Home commits a
particularly disgusting crime as his last killing before he is
himself shot down in an alley, pointing up the way in which
violence begets violence. He is sent to apprehend a black
woman, of whom he intends to take sexual advantage. He
finds she has left but does encounter her intended husband,
who does not know where she has gone. When he fails to
say where the deputy can find her, the officer brutally kills
him, castrates him, and forces his genitals down his throat.
The coroner's verdict is that Henry Brown has choked to
death on an undescribed substance accidentally lodged in
his throat. Even so, the deputy has gone too far, has become a political liability to the sheriff, and is fired. The
obvious fact that the man was emotionally unsuited for law
enforcement is never a factor.

The cause of the lynching in Trouble in July was
ostensibly a sexual violation, about which the white males
have been extremely inflammatory. This factor is translated into a solo murder in the case of Ganus of Place
Called Estherville. Ganus is innocently hunting rabbits.
He encounters the unattractive wife of a known paranoid
killer of blacks. She offers herself to him, in a familiar
pattern, promising not to tell, threatening him with exposure
when rejected, and keeping her promise by reporting falsely

to her vicious husband. She says a black entered their
house and grabbed her. At the time she makes this report,
she displays herself to her husband's companion. It is
typical of this type of woman as found in Caldwell that no
one cares that she is a nymphomaniac. Usually the chance
to hunt a black is eagerly seized. Both the husband and
companion doubt her story but enter into the hunt.

The issue, when Ganus is encountered and when he,
naturally, denies the accusation of molesting the woman,
becomes a matter of a black calling a white woman a liar.
The matter of white supremacy in all things is more important than the life of an individual black. Blacks are
characterized as always lying. Though the companion suggests following judicial procedure, he is shrugged off.
Ganus begs for reappraisal of the case when it becomes
clear that the man intends to kill him. This is rejected
on the grounds that a black cannot tell a white man what
to do. Ganus is killed by means of blows from an axe.
The assailant immediately says that Ganus was getting ready
to kill him. At the same time that the murderer-husband
threatens his companion to expect the same thing if he does
not support his story, he admits he thinks his wife had en-
ticed Ganus.

The psychotic need-to-kill on the part of some whites
is linked to sexual considerations--as in this case and that
of the deputy in Close to Home. The mutilation of Henry
Brown must not be considered an isolated case. When the
group of teenagers were harassing Ganus, they threatened
him with emasculation. The boys had already sufficient
consciousness of white sex-envy of blacks to tell him it would
be an advantage for him to be made sexually incapable. Any
such mutilation or maiming of blacks would be just as safe
as all the other crimes committed against them, being considered in the welfare of the general community of whites.

The matter of sexual relationships between races
will be dealt with separately, but the matter of rape, a
real and supposed crime, has to be included in the judicial
perversions related to blacks. Gus, the popular, bumbling
local politician in "The People's Choice" had to be pried
loose from a dark-skinned carnival dancer. That was
treated by the folk as an understandable indiscretion. In
Miss Mama Aimée the son of the household brutally raped a
black child and was neither prosecuted nor hospitalized. In

Claudelle Inglish, an aggressive white girl suggests that a
white man ask her to take her clothes off just as he would
ask a black girl.   It is assumed in Close to Home that the
deputy will take sexual advantage of Josene if he gets her
in jail.   However, the position of white society is like that
stated in A House in the Uplands: the blacks do all the
raping.   Further, in Trouble in July, one man suggests the
proper reaction to rape by a black would be to shoot every
black till the right one is punished.

    Comparably, in "The People's Choice" the town
marshal has as his main enforcement chore picking up
drunks in front of the black fish house.   He does this after
idly watching the maneuvers of a drunken white.   In another
area of legal second citizenry, Dude and Bessie, in Tobacco
Road, smash their car into a wagon driven by a black, killing him.   Unconcerned, they leave him for dead, saying,
blacks do get killed and there seems to be nothing to be
done about it.   It does not occur to them that they have
done anything criminal.   In Search of Bisco reports that the
sabotaging of machines in an integrated washeteria--by
putting sand in them--has as its only result the closing-
down of the place.

    The most fundamental of all rights is that of the
sanctity of one's home from other than a legally-authorized
search.   As recently as The Weather Shelter (1969), Caldwell was depicting the forceful, illegal search by white
vigilantes of a black house.   The general texture of the
legal status of blacks shows that they have no rights at all,
including this fundamental one.   Caldwell exemplifies this
repeatedly.   The legal profession, as Caldwell portrays it,
is appropriate to the society that supports it.   In "The
People vs. Abe Lathan, Colored," Lathan, who is being
wrongly prosecuted, cannot get a lawyer to represent him.
Representing blacks ruins a lawyer's reputation and does not
pay.   His case is, in fact, turned down by three lawyers.
The failure of the legal profession to provide defense and
counsel is a form of prejudgment of his case, contrary to
the theory of all our law, and it is caused by the fact that
Abe Lathan is black and that lawyers are aiding in the suppression of blacks.

    One instance to the contrary is reported in A House
in the Uplands: Ben Baxter, a young lawyer, and cousin of
a landowner who is very much a part of the suppressive

system, is resolved to take legal action to break the de
facto slavery. He determines to push a certain case involving black rights even if it ruins him. The boss of the
county, the judge, promises him that the penalty for not
doing as he says, dropping his legal aid to blacks, will be
the ruin of his legal career. Baxter has become known
among blacks and poor whites alike as a source of inexpen-
sive and helpful legal aid. On the one hand the judge tells
Baxter that he does not care to discuss matters with a
degraded lawyer who takes black clients. Baxter's respect
for stated and proper legal processes is taken as a sign of
defection from his assumed allegiance to the white race.
At this particular time, Baxter is trying to float a loan from
his decadent brother-in-law. A promise of legal cooperation
and financial assistance is used as bait to get Baxter to
stop helping black clients.

Through the fact that Baxter holds to his principles,
Caldwell shows he believes that there are people who believe
in the law and want to make it work. He also suggests
that not all the whites, like the innocent bystander to her
husband's wrong-headed ruin, Lucyanne Dunbar, know how
the system works. They can be enlightened. Even the white
supremacist judge, the political manipulator of the county,
admits to Baxter that the way blacks are treated is a way of
trying to mask inadequate governmental and social policies.
He encourages Baxter to go on helping blacks, who only need
education to earn a living like anyone else. He feels the
country has enough to support everybody. These are doubtless Caldwell's convictions as well.

Just as legal manipulation is to a very important
extent a matter of manipulation of language--decisions depending on what a certain word, as in a constitution written
centuries before, is taken to mean--so the matter of language was perceived by Caldwell as being quite important
to the manipulation of blacks. Even Troy Pickett in Summertime Island, who is only quasi-literate and certainly
anti-education, places a high premium on language in his
harassment of the black teacher, Duke. He starts on the
name. He starts with his suspicion of any black who comes
from the north. They are likely to be "stuck up." When
he discovers the man's name is Duke, this confirms his
idea. The name has regal implications, an example of just
another way of a black getting out of place. He grudgingly
accepts the explanation that the name is derived from the

city of Paducah, but he serves notice that he intends to re-
duce the status of any black who has pretensions, even if
they only relate to a name.   However, seventy-seven pages
later he is still bothered about the name, saying it is a
reason to run Duke out of town.

      Troy insists that Duke address him as mister.   When
they wrestle and Duke triumphs, part of his victory is that
Troy is forced to agree that Duke no longer has to address
Troy with that title.   Later Troy gets back to insisting on it
and promises to get even for all the omissions.   Trying to
treat the insecure, juvenile Troy as an equal, Duke starts
to tell him a joke.   He is rebuffed until he can do it properly, meaning that Duke must address Troy as mister.   Troy
uses what is evidently another common device in white-black
relationships.   He takes the unwarranted liberty of making
an examination of Duke's belongings.   He kicks the box in
which they are kept and makes sneering remarks on his
equipment and the education they reflect.   If Duke replies
or remonstrates, he will be wrong.   The demeaning, erosive,
exasperating trial-by-language is a weapon of psychological
warfare which can be used by people who have no understanding of the mechanism.

      In a similar way, a black who realizes the linguistic
dice are loaded is asked, in A House in the Uplands, if he
is unable to talk to a white.   In Georgia Boy, nonsensical
and threatening and exaggerated language is routine and
oppressive.   Just one of many examples of how, using the
leverage of the backing of a biased society, an inferior mind
can linguistically baffle another, is an incident involving
Handsome Brown's judgment that he will not need to wear
rubber boots in pursuing some task.   Mr. Stroup edgily
tells him to watch what he is saying.   This is a common
adjuration which can be taken as a signal that some insane
insistence is about to present itself.   Handsome, with long
training regarding such matters, then says he wishes he
owned them.   This is typical of the way in which Caldwell
finds whites force blacks to reverse themselves linguistically
to keep utterance in step with all the rest of the bondage.

      It is not only the ignorant and unlettered who practice
language terrorism.   The judge in Trouble in July has evidently used such rituals with his old personal servant,
Wardlow, so long that they move like skilled dancers through
the phases.   The judge, who is of that selfish-and-enlightened

group, who understand the real character of society but intend to use its immoral procedures just the same, seems
to find a weird, teasing humor in it. Wardlow, who has
experienced it for decades, pretends to be shaken but doubtless understands the bizarre, perverted crochet. The sum
of one of these colloquies is that Wardlow is condemned
for "letting" Sonny Clark rape the white girl. Wardlow
knows that the judge knows what an outrageous and stupid
remark that is, but he also knows that he is supposed to
reiterate the intemperate and unfounded remarks and does so.
When he walks away unsteadily, it is anyone's guess how
much he has to pretend to be unsteady.

     In **Place Called Estherville,** Kathyanne and her brother
speak normally, not employing the pauses and other man-
nerisms enforced as a part of white domination. The husband of her first town employer wonders how long it will be
before her utterance adopts the badges of servility. Similarly, when Ganus is captured and taunted by the teenagers,
they say his way of talking is odd. But they attack on
other language fronts. They tell him his name is peculiar.
He is made to say "sir" in speaking to any of them. They
even apply the ridiculous device of making him put "mister"
before the name of the town. Ganus's mixed parentage is
referred to. And the same is true of the quadroon, Jeff, in
The Weather Shelter. Terms which refer to color in ways
blacks do not like or which suggest that the color referred
to is undesirable are totally pervasive. Often it is just the
tone used, as Lucyanne, in **A House in the Uplands,** finds
herself realizing that, in abusing her, her husband used the
same tone as he employed with blacks. A woman in a bar
in **The Earnshaw Neighborhood** remarks that it was Lincoln
who freed the dinges. When she gets drunk, a distraught
woman gives expression to her frustration by referring to
the waiter as a nigger.

     Everyone has seen the sign, which appears most
especially in eating and drinking places, which says the
management reserves the right to restrict its patronage.
Even now that such restriction is illegal, **In Search of Bisco**
reports one owner as saying that this language reminds the
blacks just who controls the area. It is rather like the
people of Georgia electing a man governor and then lieutenant
governor and prospectively governor again who said the way to
handle racial problems is with a pick handle. When they were
exploring the country for the notes published in **Around About**

America (1963), the Caldwells noted that the Confederate
flag was flown as a sign of the racial attitudes of the ownership of restaurants, for example. A place which displayed
that flag refused food to a black man, even to take out.
Only the Yankee chain, the owner said, would sell to blacks.
Conversely, the absence of another symbol, the national flag
of the United States, over the post office in southern towns
was observed as an example of subtle indication of resentment of enforcement of a doctrine of insisting on rights for
all.

Every day's newspaper and television and radio
broadcast mentions some aspect of what might be called
the struggle for the schools.   Naturally, Caldwell was very
aware of the importance of the changes he hoped for, as
his father was before him.   An article by I. S. Caldwell,
"A School That Teaches a Community," in Survey for March
18, 1928, suggests the climate of awareness of the problems
of education and their significance out of which Erskine
wrote.   The elder Caldwell was reporting on a Rosenwald
school (something many southerners hated, both for the
Jewish donor of the funds involved and its aid to blacks)
at Keysville, near Wrens.   He describes how one I. E.
Bryon has gone to the town and done things which are
reminiscent of activities of more recent Peace Corps programs.   At the time of writing, steering a middle course
between "Negro indifference and undercover white hostility,"
Bryon has managed, through Rosenwald funds and other help,
to arrange to build a new school.   The board hopes to have
lumber for desks soon; in the meantime, the children use
boxes, chairs, and benches from home.   After describing
the very practical, un-academic programs involved, geared
to teaching the blacks to grow vegetables and then can them,
the Rev. Caldwell writes, "If there were enough Bryons to
man all the schools in Georgia, the proverbial 'bad Negro'
would soon be a thing of the past.   The white man is beginning to see that ignorance on the part of the Negro farmer
is the greatest hindrance to the economic development of
the state. "

It is obvious to the reader that Margaret Bourke-
White, Caldwell's collaborator on You Have Seen Their Faces
and Say: Is This the U. S. A. ?, had ideas much like his.
She spoke on the radio program, "Town Meeting," on Decem-
ber 8, 1941, on the topic, "What Must We Do to Improve the
Health and Well-being of the American People?"   After

discussing the minimal circumstances which she had seen
and which are vividly depicted in the two books she co-
authored with Caldwell, she said that the white children had
the advantage over the blacks, in that they were provided
with transportation. The blacks she had seen rarely had a
bus. She had observed schools which did not have a building
in which to meet. Classes for blacks she had seen often
met in churches, where the children sat in pews, read out-
moded texts, and lacked writing materials. They might
well be sitting under an incongruous sign inviting them to
prayer and salvation. The attitude of the whites, she found,
was that the blacks do not need education. If half of the
blacks would drop out of school, they suggested, the re-
maining teachers could be paid the higher salaries people
thought they should get. That is, they could be paid the
same salaries as whites. Caldwell and Bourke-White deemed
it a failure of democracy when blacks paid the same taxes
as whites but got decreased benefits. They had collaborated
in captioning a picture of eighteen children in a crude schoolroom in Soso, Mississippi (in Say: Is This the U.S.A.?,
1940), that they wondered at times why the schools of the
whites were so much better than theirs.

    In writing about Atlanta in In Search of Bisco (1965),
Caldwell noted that it had the best black educational facilities
in the country. He pointed out that it was forced by the
whites to be segregated. Efforts running into 1973 to provide integrated education in the Atlanta system have run into
the same maneuvering as they have everywhere in the country.
Reports indicate that black leadership, to the outrage of some
other blacks, has agreed to a modification of busing in ex-
change for some black administrative posts in the public
schools. Other reports indicate that the movement out of
the center of Atlanta to suburbs, following a national pattern, has been so great that it was an important cause of
the election of a black mayor.

    The manipulation of the blacks by the whites, massive-
ly successful as it has been, has not been completely effective. And it is obvious that it has been and is being eroded,
thanks to the interest and work of people like Erskine Caldwell. Just as racial bias and insensitivity can be learned,
so can a sense of justice and fairness and concern. Caldwell had a lasting and thorough example in his father of
effectual concern for anyone in need, physically or spiritually. Racial injustice, as has been mentioned, certainly

bothered the Reverend Ira S. Caldwell. His attitude and concern were frequently mentioned in the newspaper column he wrote. In March, 1931, he described with great regret seeing two black children turned away hungry from a restaurant. In May of that year, he told of visiting the farm of a member of his congregation where he heard black workers were lashed. He imagined he saw blood on the man's money in the collection plate. A "big man in the Methodist church" was well-known for his brutality to black tenants. Once he savagely beat a black worker who had gone to his cabin because he was ill. I. S. went to his home and tongue-lashed him and made him help with the treatment of the injuries sustained.

In October 1931, I. S. Caldwell arranged, in his role of high school teacher, for his class to go to the county seat at Louisville to see the "noted Negro chemist," George Washington Carver. In his column of October 7, 1931, he commended the gift by a white man of X-ray equipment to a black hospital. Though he thought slavery was an economic blunder, he tried to work in practical terms to alleviate and correct it, recognizing that it would be a long process, but he thought the change was inevitable.

Mention has already been made of the fact that Erskine went to spend his time with the chain gang instead of going to church in Wrens. He formed a friendship with a former yardboy, Roy, who had been sentenced to two years on the gang for stealing a washpot too large for him to lift. Roy was a mulatto like the Bisco of In Search of Bisco. Caldwell tells of risking punishment by smuggling food and tobacco to Roy.

There is much in Caldwell's work about the kindness of blacks to whites. In "Hours Before Eternity" there is a passage which deals with a kind of work-bondage of the narrator and a black woman. After the narrator has worked all day, he is told he will have to prepare his own food, being given the makings and being allowed the use of a stove. The black woman, though fearful of the boss, helps when his back is turned. In "Man and Woman" a brown woman gives help to a starving white woman but not to her husband. She offers the comment that the woman's husband should be of more help to her. "The Visitor" uses a memory of an old black man sucking the poison out of a bee sting as a start of an episode of love-making. In "Wild

Flowers, " after hesitating, blacks take into their home a
desperately-needy white man.   They let him use their cart
to get his wife's body.   A paralyzed worker, who has been
injured while working with blacks, is the central figure of
"A Knife to Cut the Cornbread. " The blacks have helped
him when the owner would not. The anxiety-crazed para-
lytic begs a knife which is ostensibly to be used for cornbread, but actually he has the idea, presented in the story
only in prospect, of cutting his own flesh for food.   The
black, incidentally, refers to the hypocritical church-goer
who will not help as Mr. Jesus.

        Summertime Island has several factors relating to
friendly black-white relationships.   Guthry decides to take
Duke on the fishing trip in preference to several whites who
wanted to go.   Thus he has to put up with the others' juvenile and jealous remarks, asking whether Duke will sleep
in the same tent, for example.   Another says he would
trade the male for a female partner.   The narrator, who
has aspects of Caldwell in him, is a young boy.   Perhaps
recollections of his young days in Tennessee might have
contributed to Caldwell's forming of this character.   He and
Duke clean and eat fish together and go swimming together.
A more intense relationship than the friendship of Duke and
the young boy, Steve, is seen in the love of Grover for his
son, Jeff, in The Weather Shelter.   Grover, well-to-do
owner of a pony farm, is deeply attracted to a mulatto
woman, whom he wants to marry.   His lawyer convinces
him he can not do that.   The white man and the brown
woman follow the inclination of their feelings, and a child
is born.   The woman is killed by a madly-possessive black,
who wants to marry her and use her for prostitution.   The
boy learns late in his teens who his father is when the latter
saves him from lynching.   The love of the white father for
the quadroon son is deep and explicit and sadly hampered
by the limitations of society.

        The sheriff in Trouble in July has little to recommend
him.   It is true he means no harm.   But he means so little
good that it is an extremely bad joke for him to be sheriff.
But it is a partial palliative that he has a genuine friendship for, and interest in, Sam, who keeps selling mortgaged
cars and keeps spending time in jail.   He is there when the
frustrated lynchers storm into the jail, looking for some
kind of satisfaction.   They express their bitterness by taking
Sam along as hostage.   If Sonny Clark is not found, they

will have someone to lynch. The sheriff is almost as useless in regard to helping Sam as he is in everything else,
but he really does care what happens to him. He bumbles
about the countryside at length, quite a sacrifice for a man
with his limited capacity for action. He hopes quite hard
that Sam will be set free. The lynchers know that he has
had orders to stay out of the area, but he blunders about
and has the inconvenience of encountering them while hoping
to run into Sam. His interest in Sam is great enough to
cause him to jeopardize his intense need to keep the lynching
"politically clean." He really concentrates on Sam, rather
than Sonny, whom he should rescue from the lynchers. Sam,
who has been chased through thickets with a rope around his
neck and been forced to run tied behind a car, part of the
time being dragged along the ground, is released when Sonny
is found. The sheriff stumbles across him and takes him
back to the jail. It is a study in minor, ineffectual decency.
Also on a minor scale, but not without significance, is the
attitude of the white guest in The Earnshaw Neighborhood
(1971), who says placing another guest in a separate
room will only make more work for the maid and requests
therefore to share with the other.

          Two episodes were very important to Caldwell in the
matter of being helped by blacks. He gives two different
versions of how a black prisoner in the jail smuggled out a
message for him when he was, unaccountably, being held
incommunicado. But they both center on the same thing.
The black risks a lot to help him. He certainly would have
been punished if the jailer had known. As it is, Ramey,
the black, says the best way Caldwell can repay him for
his good deed is to make certain no one knows. Caldwell
waited thirty years to write anything about it. A very significant case of being rescued by a good Samaritan occurred
when Caldwell was fifteen and working as a driver for the
YMCA director at Millington Field, near his home in Atoka,
Tennessee. He was to drive the director's car from Clarks-
dale to Memphis. In a thunderstorm the Ford he was driving
overturned in a ditch. He was pinned in it and might have
been drowned by rising water, but he was found by Troy, a
black farmer, who took him to his home and cared for him.
He awoke to find himself in a bed in the black man's home.
Caldwell shows in his writing that he knows that the vastly-
needed changes in society are not only possible but also
some have even happened.

IV. THE CHARACTER OF BLACKS

Erskine Caldwell's mother, who was from Virginia, observed, while he was still a child, that the blacks were not yet able to stand alone. In need of guidance, support and instruction, the blacks, she thought, had a child-like simplicity and were still dependent on the people who had enslaved them. She was doubtless confused by the role of obsequiousness which generations of experience had taught the blacks would satisfy the whites. Caldwell's descriptions of the older blacks in Summertime Island and In Search of Bisco refer to elderly blacks sitting in front of a store and doffing their hats as the whites pass. They would also bow or back away, hat in hand. They had learned to grovel in feigned cheerfulness. Trouble in July contains a reference to the hardworking, amiable black.

Experienced blacks learned to use self-deprecating language, even when doggedly insisting on a point, even when the effort was obviously doomed from the start. This kind of verbal warfare is well exemplified in A House in the Uplands. The owner is irascible and tyrannical with his servants, who are outwardly the very models of submission. They compliment him elaborately on his not firing them from their non-job. In Georgia Boy, Handsome Brown always plays straight whatever mind-boggling insistence presents itself. Mrs. Stroup, who is trying to cope with the fact that her husband has stolen a calf, tells Handsome to leave and cautions him to silence, noting that he will be telling lies for himself if he is not careful. Handsome replies that he has always tried to do what either of the Stroups has told him.

This is to be differentiated from the linguistic tyranny mentioned earlier, in which, as in the case of the relationship of the judge and Wardlow in Trouble in July, the white man uses language to rule the black in his bondage. Wardlow is younger than the judge, but he looks a great deal older. The judge is upset and worried about the

reported rape and the impending lynching. The judge shouts
that he should send Wardlow to hell for letting this event
happen. Wardlow offers never to complain again over any
action of the judge if he may be spared the fiery furnace.
In the rest of the colloquy, though in an extreme state of
excitement and fear, Wardlow abases himself by denouncing
himself in terms as close as possible to those used by the
judge. The effort to say so completely what he does not
believe or mean or deserve leaves him leaning against the
wall, but he does it.

      Even though they had been taught to fear whites, the
blacks maintained a posture of controlled expression. In
their position of hated-object-of-fear, they walked a chalk
line to express themselves while at the same time avoiding
giving any excuse for retaliation, which could be expected
to be violent and harmful if not fatal.

      Thus an older black particularly might be expected
to have mastered circumlocution, circling around the target,
seeming not even to be shooting at it, but attacking it just
the same. Here, paraphrased, is an example from In
Search of Bisco: It is against my nature to say anything
bad about anyone. And I don't mean to say anything against
any white folks. Probably what they are doing is right.
But I don't see how it is right. If it is right, I don't see
how it is right. At least, I don't see yet how it is right.
It does not seem right to kill somebody for breaking a hoe
handle and then drop the body in a well and not have anybody do anything about it. I do not expect anybody to be
treated like that.

      Evading saying exactly what one wants to say while
still leaving the inevitable suggestion of it requires skill.
And so does being a self-controlled servant, keeping out of
the disasters of those one works for. The predicament of
Hubert in "August Afternoon" is illustrative: Mr. Vic, for
whom Hubert works, has married a promiscuous nymphet.
Mr. Vic is afraid to interfere when a stranger, Floyd,
approaches, receives encouragement, and openly cuckolds
Mr. Vic with Willie, the girl-wife-nymphomaniac. Mr.
Vic tries to put Hubert in the middle, frustratedly asking
him to interfere. Hubert has forethoughtedly disposed of
a gun Mr. Vic asks him to get and use. Hubert displays
throughout that he has thought about ways to avoid the
dangers of being entangled in the difficulties of "white folks."

Martha uses classic black tactics of evasion in A
House in the Uplands. She pretends not to understand and
not to remember, in one case to protect a white woman
whom she likes from indignity and injury. She tries to
give advice evasively for veiled reasons. The truth, which
is explosive, is admitted to partially and reluctantly. She
sorrowfully asks not to be questioned further. She then reveals the truth, stipulating that she does it because she is
required to. She comments on how she has tried to evade
problems of whites and sees that the devil is forcing her
into this one. She also makes reference to the fact that
she has futilely warned a quadroon that her association with
the white owner will lead to disaster.

In Georgia Boy, Handsome Brown, being entrusted
with the contraband information that Pa Stroup has gone
fishing, something Mrs. Stroup would not approve, has a
problem when Mrs. Stroup tackles him about it. When he
is first asked if he knows where Mr. Stroup is, he does
not answer. Then he is specifically told to answer when
addressed. He counters by asking if Mr. Stroup is "around."
He is reminded that there would be no inquiry if he were
and is indignantly criticized for beating around the bush.
Pretending that he does not understand the figure of speech,
Handsome says he is not doing that to any bushes. To a
direct request that Mrs. Stroup be told where Mr. Stroup
went, Handsome offers the speculation that he might have
gone to the barber's, for he needed a haircut. She im-
patiently reiterates that she wants the truth. Replying that
he is really making an effort to supply it, he suggests that
he might have gone to the sawmill for some lumber. Mrs.
Stroup glances at the place where Mr. Stroup's fishing pole
is not. Handsome volunteers that Mr. Stroup had said he
was going to look at some calves. Mrs. Stroup wants to
know why he took the fishing pole. Handsome suggests he
might have changed his mind, thinking that it was not a good
time to look at calves. Thoroughly exasperated with Handsome, Mrs. Stroup says it is not a good time to tell lies
and heads for the house. Feeling he has now made her
angry, Handsome follows her and explains that the lie was
for Mr. Stroup, not for himself. Because he always tries
to do what he is told and is pulled in two different directions,
he finds it hard to be truthful to two opposing authorities at
once.

In A House in the Uplands, Beckum, who is used to

dodging verbal and other brickbats, tries to deliver a message while his owner is belaboring his wife. Overpowered
by the intense reaction to his appearance, he leaves without giving the message. Ten pages later, he finally gets
across the fact that a man is waiting to see the owner.

        Black servants in The Weather Shelter, Della and
Annie, tread softly on the margin of an erupting domestic
volcano. Madge Danford, the woman of the house, has
suddenly decided to declare the homosexual aspect of her life
by bringing her female lover, Mickey Pete, home with her.
Her unsuspecting husband, who has always believed the explanation that her many trips to the city were for medical
treatment, has, in the initial stages of the scene, not
learned of the "friend" who has accompanied his wife. As
Della and Annie observe the situation, their normal friend-
liness turns into humorless efficiency. When the husband,
Grover, tries to get them into conversation, they do not
respond. Finally, Annie cryptically comments that Madge
has company. Questioned as to who it is, Annie at first
shrugs and then says she does not think Grover would like
to know the person. She adds, when quizzed further, she
does not know how to say more and that he will have to
draw his own conclusions. Grover is shaken by this vague,
secret menace; he still has no suspicion of his wife's relationship to the guest. The blacks do not, of course, want
to have any more connection than is necessary with the
very distasteful development.

        Shortly after, in the midst of an emotional scene in
the dining room between Grover, Madge and Micky Pete,
the servants soundlessly bring in breakfast for the two
women. In this confrontation, Madge aggressively makes
clear that she no longer intends to remain married to
Grover, and she prepares to leave with her companion. The
servants, who have heard everything, including references to
the husband's love affair with a half-white woman, smile
and hum as they go about their work. As usual, the blacks
have known everything and have commented on the events
while saying practically nothing.

        The evasive-but-distinct expressions take many forms.
Josene in Close to Home persists in calling a newly-married
widow by her former name. The reason is that the woman
has married her lover. But she just "forgets." Lucyanne
in A House in the Uplands is bothered by the fact that,

though the servants have always been respectful and agreeable, they have left an indefinable impression of not accepting
her. The lateness of a school teacher is caused by the lateness of her servant, who has used her own standard of time
as a way of insisting on her own way. In Summertime Island, there is a very important wrestling match between a
black and a white. It is noted that such a confrontation is
unusual. Usually the black will back off; shooting and
knifing are more to be expected, it is pointed out. Probably a more unusual (and dubious) form of evasion is reported in "Hours Before Eternity": a man tries to abduct
a black girl, but she has greased her body with lard and
escapes.

Outlets other than language are used to express black
feelings. Their silence has a variety of manifestations. In
Summertime Island, three different blacks have been invited
to go on a camping trip that will include a bigoted white
deliveryman. They have presented various excuses, but he,
probably rightly, thinks they are lying. He suspects that
they have decided not to cooperate with him because he always drops what he delivers to them in the street. He feels
no white man should meet black expectations when making a
delivery. They evidently feel they do not have to tell him
why they will not go.

A black who engages in bootlegging and has been
arrested a great many times on that account finally makes
a deal with the police that he will spend each night in the
jail. This incredible arrangement has one very satisfactory
aspect from the point of view of the black. He has become
the only black to sleep in the center of town, out of the
segregated black area. As long as no one says anything
about it, the whimsical arrangement can continue. Whether
this is drawn from life or is just Caldwell's translation of
how grotesque relations between the races can be may only
be guessed.

In A House in the Uplands, a white woman approaches
the cabin area of the blacks on a plantation. She is looking
for her husband, who is visiting his mistress in one of the
cabins. As the woman proceeds into the area, the music
and laughter and talk cease. She is watched in silent ap-
prehension of unhappy events to come. Later in the same
book, the blacks congregate in fearful silence as spectators
to the scene after the owner has been shot by a gambler.

Handsome Brown, in Georgia Boy, sees trouble approaching
in the form of a female selling ties.   He simply stops in
silence with his spoon half way to his mouth.   Also, Handsome Brown believes it does not pay to enter into conversa-
tions with gypsies.   In Trouble in July, after the search
for Sonny Clark has started, all black cabins are silent,
and the roads are deserted by the blacks.   As an overall
commentary on a way of life which contained many silences,
In Search of Bisco records the remark of the long-time
yardboy to the effect that he envies the younger people,
who speak out.

       In two of his books, Caldwell uses song as a means
of indirect expression.   The blacks in the cabins in A
House in the Uplands sing a concert of appropriate blues
songs as the sexual and racial relationship between the
people in the main house and those in the cabins is played
out.   A woman sings a song of troubled and frustrated love;
it floats through the window to intensify the suffering of the
owner's wife.   In God's Little Acre, Black Sam and Uncle
Felix orchestrate the problems of the Waldens with appropriate blues songs, commenting on the situation.   The songs
are a way of commenting without personal involvement.   The
music may be received or ignored as most songs are not
related to the personal circumstances of those who hear
them.   This gives the blacks a way of knowing and commenting but avoiding person-to-person involvement--intent can
be suspected but not proved.   The function is reminiscent
of the chorus in Greek drama.

       Similar is the guitar-playing, which at times accom-
panies the singing; it also provides a commentary, with
emphasis, on what is happening, without directly saying anything to anyone.   As Lucyanne's husband goes to the black
quarter in A House in the Uplands, he hears a song with
guitar accompaniment about a bad woman taking a good
woman's man.   In that book, too, the mood of the guitar
music changes with the situation, serving to underline or
summarize what is happening.   The guitar is sad and ten-
tative, for example, when Lucyanne makes her voyage of
discovery to the black quarter.

       Laughter is another adroit and impersonal means of
expression which can be explicit.   On one occasion, in A
House in the Uplands, guitar-playing and laughter are combined to provide an insistent accompaniment to Lucyanne's

own feeling. Laughter accompanies the music of abandon-
ment. The young, aggressive woman to whom Lucyanne's
husband goes laughs derisively in the black quarter. In a
critical vein, a black woman watches, in The Sure Hand of
God, a frantic minister's wife take off her clothes, run out
in the backyard, and curse. The maid laughs uproariously
at the frustration of her employer. In another way of com-
menting-without-words, the white woman, Lucyanne, as depicted in A House in the Uplands, finding her husband un-
repentantly involved with his confident quadroom mistress,
leaves the black quarter conscious of the muffled voices of
the blacks, discussing her and her situation. As has been
variously suggested already, the whites, in depending so in-
timately and completely on the blacks, opened themselves up
completely to their observation. And, just as black comments were made in a subdued and indirect way, so it was
that white reaction found voice in open and frank statements.
It has been seen that some of the utterances of blacks led
to the most devastating of reprisals.

As an interpolation to the narrative of The Last Night
of Summer, a black points out that white people use vulgar
language and that the females do most of it. The man says
he could not accept the way white women criticize their men
in front of others. The practice offends his sense of propriety. He intends to continue to earn his living by performing services for them, but he is glad he does not have
to associate with them otherwise. He is glad that his "place"
is different from that of whites.

Though they do not play a significant role in the book,
blacks are used by Caldwell to comment on the level of life
of the Lesters in Tobacco Road. Several blacks form an
audience to the antics at the Lester cabin, of Lov and Ellie
May in particular. Dude is bothered by them and shouts
epithets at them. The blacks are reported to have discussed
the Lesters scornfully, but they address Lov respectfully.
When he does not reply, being preoccupied with Ellie May,
they do not address him again. The blacks continue to watch
the bizarre scene. When the family overpower Lov, Dude
is sufficiently conscious of the blacks that he speculates
they will try to help Lov; Dude thereupon prepares to attack
them. As interested as they may have been in trying to
help Lov, they were more interested in what might happen
next to Ellie May. The whites were, as they must continually have been, a source of entertainment to the blacks,

and the subject of a good deal of discussion.

In God's Little Acre, too, the blacks have a witness
role. They watch the chaotic degradation of the whites.
Ty Ty realizes he can not hide the disastrous situation from
the blacks. Black Sam says, after Will Thompson is shot,
that the death of the "male man" is bound to effect the
women. This comment, touching on sex and white women,
is a little too overt. Thus, when Ty Ty demands an explanation, Black Sam retreats into saying that he meant
nothing. But, after Ty Ty has left, Black Sam and Uncle
Felix make a kind of patter of their appreciation of the
charms of Darling Jill, saying essentially the same thing
Ty Ty had said. Generally speaking, they seem to enjoy
the white catastrophe and have a lot to say about it. The
two blacks are used to forecast more trouble in the last
chapter. Grandma Maddox, in Close to Home, seems at
first to be one of the conservative blacks who believe in
going along with the dominating system. She tries to keep
Henry Brown from saying the things about his rights that
enraged a deputy so much that Henry is killed and mutilated.
Then she expresses her repugnance for what life has held
for her as a black by saying that she wants to be buried
lying on her face so that she can no longer see what happens on earth. When she says that the whites are dominant
and privileged, she is told that changes are coming.

Other writings are speckled with comments on whites.
Jeff, a black in A House in the Uplands, slyly and politely
says that the owner of the plantation is certainly a fine person but that he does not like blacks, except when he is
interested in quadroon women. Then he waits to see if the
poor white farmer he is talking to disapproves. A waiter
in The Last Night of Summer, after noting the vulgar way
the woman which he has served has swilled down her drink,
says he would not stay in a family which included such a
woman. Zerena, in The Earnshaw Neighborhood, is quite
outspoken. She comments on the varying moods of the
police. Sometimes they are aggressive and sometimes they
are eager to please. When she is told to put her employer's
husband in the guest room, she comments on the fact that
the two do not sleep together. Another time she tells her
employer she is amazed at the way whites act. The black
matron in the White Turkey brothel, in Tragic Ground, expresses her scorn of good-for-nothing white trash. In
Trouble in July, the wife of Sam, the man who was abducted

as a stand-by to be used, if necessary, in the lynching,
asks a white when will the whites leave the blacks alone.

The white child, Vearl, in Journeyman, has syphilis.
Susan, the black woman with whose family Vearl lives, has
asked Vearl's father repeatedly to get him treated. She disliked the disease for the child and was afraid of contamina-
tion of her own. She had even tried to take him to town to
be treated, but he had broken away from her en route.
Susan did not blame the boy's father for his having the disease, but she did blame him for not getting it treated. The
boy's mother gives Susan medicine for the disease. Susan
feels she can depend on her to keep after his father until
he has been cured. Zerena White is a person of truly
doughty spirit and free expression. She is one of the few
persons who can get the better of her white employer,
Medora Earnshaw, who gives her name to the neighborhood
for which the Earnshaw book is named. She insists on being
called Mrs. White and will not work otherwise. If Medora
forgets, she has to make the correction. Zerena tells
Medora to wear clothes more suitable to her age; Medora
complains about her frank expression. Zerena says that
the time she has had to waste talking has interfered with
her work. She suggests she might quit. When Medora
says not to mention that idea, she says she will stop mentioning it but will keep it in mind. Characteristically,
when she is told to call the police, she suggests that
Medora do it. When Medora's husband gets too frisky, she
threatens to tell his wife about him. She orders him out
of the kitchen and tells him he is crazy when he starts to
sing. Zerena will not let her daughter model in a club
because it is not integrated.

Evidently, the minister's wife, Christine, in The
Sure Hand of God, fears the comments of her maid. She
makes sure to get home before dawn so that her maid will
not know she has been out all night. After her husband has
been shot the night before, in Journeyman, Susan says the
event did not bother her. The implication is that everyone
expects to listen to her legitimate complaint. She explains
by saying she is not going to complain. Caldwell gives,
in Miss Mama Aimée, an example of a servant's having a
hand in controlling her situation: she complains about the
way dinner must be served and wants the time changed.
She, like others mentioned, is not afraid to speak up.

Martha, of A House in the Uplands, has lived a long

time with the deck stacked against the blacks. She sees
the quadroon, Sallie, playing with the owner of the plantation, as headed for disaster. So she tries, futilely, to dis-
courage her notions of freedom and power. Acting like a
free woman, she feels, will only attract problems for her.
Martha also acts as maid-confidante to the leading white
female in the book, fiftyish and tearful. She tried to help
the abandoned and degraded young wife with what her half-
a-dozen common law marriages have taught her. What she
offers only makes the woman feel worse, and she is dis-
missed sharply. Handsome Brown's suggestions are at times
so unwelcome that on one occasion he was threatened with
being put on the chain gang.

  The fact that blacks are everywhere makes it only
natural that they should commonly be called upon as sources
of information. Handsome Brown supplies information as to
how a fight started between two baseball teams. A black
servant is the family news-provider in Miss Mama Aimée.
And there are many other examples of cases in which a black
provides an interesting or useful piece of information.

  A rare but indicative example of black expression
and creativity is the character Sam, a hotel shoeshine boy,
whom Caldwell puts in The Last Night of Summer. He
makes up and sings his own songs. He does this to avoid
dependence on what the juke box has to offer. He has
plenty of material, both happy and sad, about which to write.
Caldwell not only gives him the power of linguistic and
musical creativity, additionally he gives him credit for
shrewd observations. The song he is currently singing is
about a tan-skinned girl who wanted a man and then shot
him down when she got tired of him. He can not say why
a woman would do that. He has avoided being shot by being
alert about when a woman was about to get rid of him.
His advice is to accept pleasant treatment and to keep on
the watch constantly. The danger sign is when the woman
becomes impossible to please. Something within the woman
turns to ice. He does not intend to get careless about the
matter. Having said that, quite unusual for someone giving
a shine, he proceeds to observe that his client seems to be
getting ready to enter a new relationship with a woman.
Caldwell thus allows him to bring forth a key consideration
in the book.

  Whereas Zerena in The Earnshaw Neighborhood

discussed quitting her job, negotiations in Miss Mama Aimée
do not produce the desired results. Thus Martha announces
that she is going to work for another employer. The very
free discussion following ranges over a variety of subjects,
making it clear that Caldwell feels there are black employees
in the Sixties who no longer fear the "white cross people"
and are willing to comment on the family situation just as
they see it.

As long as the blacks had been in captivity, they had
tried to leave it. The arrangements in this century to keep
black workers tied to their posts, no matter how unsatisfactory or unrewarding, have been mentioned earlier. Thus
the desire and ability to move freely away from a job, as
Martha does, is important. For Handsome Brown, leaving
the Stroups is the pot of gold at the end of the rainbow. He
knows the girl selling ties will cause trouble, and he wishes
he had the dishes done so that he could take his day off.
He avoids the convict-relative. He did run away once (to
become the target in a carnival baseball pitch) because, he
said, he was tired of working for nothing and having his
banjo taken by Mr. Stroup. He has no hard feelings but
is tired of it. Though he wants pay instead of old clothes
and other hand outs, he returns when Mr. Stroup hits him
three-out-of-three with the baseball. There is no negotia-
tion about the banjo, either.

Sometimes a simple change in the state of a part of
the body will say all that needs to be said. In Summertime
Island, Troy goes to try to enjoy the favor of the daughter
of the owner of a boat he is to ride in. Duke is "wide-
eyed with anxiety." Duke finally has to wrestle Troy and
beat him to wring concessions from him. Troy has to
agree, for the time being, not to order Duke around. Lee,
the bouncer in The Last Night of Summer, does not have to
say anything to customers who want to mistreat the girls.
He has developed a special hold, involving the arm and the
crotch, for this purpose. When Zerena becomes exasperated at Medora's husband, she strikes him. When Josene
is angry in the kitchen, in Close to Home, she bangs pots
and kettles. Wardlow, in Trouble in July, bangs the door
when the sheriff leaves.

Demonstrations are mentioned by Caldwell in Around
About America and In Search of Bisco. He notes that they
can only be carried on successfully in the cities. He sees,

too, that they are the result of the fact that blacks have found freedom of expression. The record of how Caldwell saw the blacks as expressing themselves has shown that they did it with variety and vitality. Even more illuminating are the attitudes he records them as expressing, in either words or deeds. Considering all the emphasis placed on the work-role of the blacks in the agricultural economy of the south, it is not surprising he has a man remark in Trouble in July that the Geechees will do anything to get out of the fields. And that doubtless goes for any others as well. A man who had managed to work and save and accumulate a house and a little store appears in In Search of Bisco. He has worked hard and probably well. Uncle Jeff Davis Fletcher, in Georgia Boy, is a specialist. He is the custodian of the Universalist Church. When Morris Stroup and his young son try to take his place, they sound the death knell and break up the wedding. As everyone says, Uncle Jeff would have done it right.

Caldwell knows that the natural desires of blacks to live as well as possible work against the adverse circumstances that surround them and which they have been trained to accept. In Search of Bisco quotes a farm worker who finds the white landlord wants to keep him in a degraded state of life in the Mississippi delta. He informs the landlord that, like it or not, he is going to New Jersey to work in a factory. He has been there, knows that conditions are not perfect, but sees a great improvement in what he can achieve there.

Chapter Four of Deep South is devoted to the improved possibilities for blacks and contains two monologues by young blacks, one a professional football prospect and the other a student of history. The second has some very forthright things to say about how he finds blacks will discriminate against blacks, as in a nightclub, seating him away from the best tables, because he is black. It is to be understood that black ambition has nothing new about it. In God's Little Acre mention is made of the way the blacks, low as their status is in that book, are also digging for gold, behind their cabins and all over the county, all the time.

Writing in his Augusta, Georgia, newspaper column, in 1931, Erskine's father gives an admiring account of a black doctor performing a major operation and saving a life. Noting that "only yesterday" all those who aided in the opera-

tion were savages, he expresses his appreciation of the skill
of the doctor and the intelligence of the nurses.   He tells
his readers that there is probably not another case in history where a people had made as much progress so fast as
the blacks.   He takes the occasion to say that, in spite of
unwise white leadership, he thinks racial hatred will eventually disappear.

In the course of his New School lectures in January,
1938, Erskine had offered the opinion that the blacks had
more independence and capacity to survive then whites in
corresponding situations.   He used In Search of Bisco to
record his observation that the younger blacks were growing up without the fear that had tended to immobilize their
elders.   As early as in "Squire Dinwiddy" he had known that
a black could be a go-getter.   Dinwiddy goes to work for
a family in Connecticut as a man of all work.   However,
after three weeks he has to leave.   It seems he has to fly
to Washington to collect rent on tenements he owns there.
He has to collect rents on time in order to avoid losses
caused by eviction action.   He has the attitude of the most
materialistic of landlords.

A black maid in The Last Night of Summer orders
food for a special party, giving explicit orders to a waiter,
telling him she will share the tip if he does well.   He replies she did not give him much of it the last time.   Her
tart rejoinder is that he might get less.   Duke, in Summertime Island, hungers for independence to travel; thus he is
not ready to marry.   He expresses his chafing at all the
restraints of being black by saying he wants to have all the
freedom of movement that a large catfish in the river has.
In You Have Seen Their Faces there is a picture of a black
farmer in Arlington, Tennessee, who owns a fifty-three-
acre farm with a five-room house, a pasture, a garden,
and a complement of animals.   A black organizer of a Boy
Scout troop, in In Search of Bisco, insisted that each ghetto
boy have at least one item of the uniform.   When the husband of her employer starts to approach Kathyanne in Place
Called Estherville, he begins to tell her about savings accounts.   She briskly tells him she already has one.

The fullest expression of black independence of spirit
is found in Zerena White, of The Earnshaw Neighborhood
(1971), a mulatto with Indian blood.   She and her husband,
a carpenter, have a well-kept home in Dingy Flat.   Medora

Earnshaw, her employer, offers to give an old dress to
Zerena, who promptly rejects it, saying it can be used for
a duster when the present supply of old rags is exhausted.
Zerena suggests that guests, who are causing too much work,
should move out. When Medora says she hopes other people
do not have discontented servants, Zerena replies that they
will not if the help does what she intends to do, stop working as soon as possible. Suze, one of Zerena's three daughters, is nineteen; her tan color and voluptuous figure have
won a beauty contest for her, and she is saving her money
to go to a modeling school in Atlanta. Suze walks around
the house naked, hoping to learn better how to display her
figure; this makes Zerena doubtful about taking her into the
Earnshaw house. When it becomes convenient for her, however, Zerena informs Medora that Suze will take her place.
In the ultimate contrast to the manner of plantation blacks,
she does not ask if she may have the time off. She simply
announces it will not suit her to come in. She is going to
work on her burial lot. Suze will not wear a maid's uniform. She will dress any way she wants to.

   Medora is described as enjoying Zerena's domination,
and is happy that she has more sense than to fire her.
She seems to have no inkling of the social history which
lies behind the insistences of Zerena, but her particular
personality enjoys being under Zerena's control, just as she
enjoys making her husband and daughter do her will.
Medora has never heard of such independence from a black
woman; she wonders about it and admires and appreciates
it. Zerena is, of course, entirely competent, as she knows,
in her handling of Medora, a rather complicated, impulsive
person.

   Another aspect of Caldwell's understanding of black
independence would have come from a family episode dating
back to when they lived in Prosperity, S.C. (from 1906 to
1911). An illiterate black Baptist minister had the habit of
getting every week from Erskine's father a text and an explanation of it for his use in his service on Sunday. One
Saturday night he called for his usual help, only to find,
to his dismay, that his benefactor was absent. However,
Mrs. Caldwell agreed to help, giving him the text orally and a
simple explanation of its meaning the next morning. When
the delighted minister thanked her, he remarked, "I'll just
go now and improve on this before I preach the sermon."
In Search of Bisco says that segregation in religion is

important to many blacks. Even though they do not like the
isolation, it is necessary for them to improve themselves
on their own, to do things their own way. The absence of
literacy and information in general has been a great and
calculated burden for the blacks. You Have Seen Their Faces
carried a picture of a very large, probably pregnant, black
woman, who is sitting on the steps of a cabin with a baby
in her arms and another small child nearby. Having more
children than she can handle already, she is quoted as likening the coming of children to the growth of watermelon.
For many years and continuingly, blacks and others who
care about them and the society of which they are a part
have known that more and freer education for them is essential. Caldwell uses In Search of Bisco to enunciate this
point.

        In Say: Is This the U.S.A.? he and Margaret Bourke-
White have a black school principal relating that his people
do not get their just due in education. He is paid fifty dollars a month, one of his teachers, forty, and the rest,
twenty-five dollars. The range of salaries in the white
school is from a hundred to two hundred dollars. White
teachers can advance themselves by summer study, but
blacks can not afford it. Black teachers depend on gifts
for food and lodging. The principal says he does not envy
the whites anything that they have but wants the same for
blacks. As he has to report it, they get books and equipment by taking up a collection. When he asks for equal
funds, people say the blacks do not need much education.
A picture of a school scene in the same book shows children
sitting in a poorly-equipped room. The caption notes that
the children do not have sports equipment, because their
parents can barely supply them even with necessities. At
the same time, the blacks, as the people In Search of Bisco
mention, want their children to get as much education as
possible, and they have to withstand the discouragement and
antagonism of biased whites.

        Around About America (1964) avers that children in
the south are taught bias in the schools. The Confederate
flag is a symbol of it. Racial disturbances, Caldwell finds,
are often related to activities of students in secondary and
higher schools. Caldwell uses the relationship between the
black teacher, Duke, and the white bigot, Troy, to emphasize this point in Summertime Island (1968). Troy's sadistic attitude toward blacks is rooted in his lack of education.

Duke saves Troy from drowning. Troy's only comment is
to note how pleased the "educated black" is over his ac-
complishment, suggested to be rare. Earlier, Troy had told
Duke he hoped his education had been good enough to keep the
liquor bottles from breaking, a skill Troy would deem important.

Doubtless there is a relationship between limited
education and lack of sexual restraint. The stereotype of
the black is that sex with them is unrestrained. Martha
Bell, the maid in Episode in Palmetto, portrays the empty-
headed, amorous, loquacious type. Knockout Harris, the
fighter in Poor Fool, is aggressive and even vicious in his
sexual reactions. He boasts, too, that he fathers twins
"about half the time." In Journeyman, Semon Dye is able
to bring around the reluctant Susan by patting her buttocks.
She looks around helplessly as she is drawn into a house.
Suze, the girl who wants to be a model, responds favorably
to petting, which outrages her mother, Zerena.

Kathyanne, who has to submit, does so with infinite
dignity in Place Called Estherville. When her employer's
husband approaches her, she tells him she is a good girl.
When he reaches for her she calmly asks him if color makes
a difference. Caldwell uses the episode to show the weakness, really the inferiority, of the white attitude. As she
calmly and contemptuously looks at the man who is preparing
to take advantage of her, he falls back on the idea which has
been used long and widely by whites; he feels superior because he is white. As he presses against her, he tells her
white girls are not to couple with blacks. She says she
knows of this attitude, not commenting on its acceptability.
She also says that she will not tell his wife of his behavior
but will have to leave their employ. Telling her that it
will be her own fault, he feels he has to overcome her or
feel he has been faced down by a mulatto. The reader is
left to imagine whether he has his way with her, but there
is no doubt which of the two is the more mature person.
The need of the white man to bolster his damaged ego is
related to the statement in Around About America that Caldwell feels the whites envy the blacks their supposed greater
sexual attractiveness and joy of life. The sense of inferiority that goes with envy is the basis, he thinks, for ex-
pressions of negativity and cruelty by whites.

The reader will recall the drastic solution to black
exuberance in "Candy-Man Beechum," in which a man who

is just going his sweet way down the street is cut down
ruthlessly by a law officer for no reason. "Big Buck" has
as its central character an ebullient black, much like Candy-
Man, who goes a-wooing with verve and playfully intimidates
other blacks less physically dominant. And "The Courting
of Susie Brown" has the atmosphere of a kind of fairy tale
in which the one who wins the king's daughter has to accom-
plish something no one could: Susie will not have just any
man (like Kate in The Taming of the Shrew), but Sampson
slyly and determinedly wins her after all.

What Caldwell has to say about blacks is that they
are people just like anyone else. One of his most telling
ways of doing so was the inclusion in You Have Seen Their
Faces of the picture of a small, bright-eyed, eight-year-old,
barefoot black boy, in tattered overalls, standing in the ex-
terior doorway of a cluttered, board-floored house with newspaper walls. Next to him is a sad-eyed hound, of whom the
child makes a lovingly-deprecating remark. The capacity to
love negates the differentiation of the trappings of poverty.
In "The Growing Season" Caldwell shows us a black who
can not stand the suffering of a starving mule. In Search of
Bisco says that blacks think of mules as "people." As they
find great joy of life in association with animals, so do they
like to fish and go to carnivals (Georgia Boy), or just sit
and doze and watch the river (You Have Seen Their Faces),
or do anything else that anyone else might.

Knowing that it is part of the ordinary view of blacks
that they are outstandingly superstitious, Caldwell has used
one story, "Nine Dollars Worth of Mumble," to attack this
stereotype. The nine dollars worth of charms or curses
extracted during the course of a failed romance is characterized as all mumble. The blacks in God's Little Acre
were, of course, as superstitious as the whites about the
gold-locating powers of an albino. Relatedly, it has long
pleased whites to think of blacks as innocent and trusting,
doubtless casting them in the docile role they see as convenient if not required. The episode in Journeyman, in
which white rascal-preacher Semon Dye approaches Susan,
throws light on what Caldwell sees. Susan knows she can
not rebel openly or violently, but she reminds Dye that her
husband will not like it if she acquiesces. Dye explains that
the case is different because he is white; she elicits from
him the fact that he is a preacher. She cynically says she
thought so and oughtn't he tend to his proper business rather

than chasing black women.   In A House in the Uplands,
there is skepticism concerning the possibility of getting
legal aid in Maguffin, the county seat.   Uncle Jeff thinks
the whites stick together when it is a matter involving
blacks.   And, in The Weather Shelter, when a white man
and his tan son inquire in the black quarter of a strange
city for the boy's grandparents, the response is both skep-
tical and fearful.

        In Deep South, Caldwell notes the blacks have little
trust in the fundamentalist religion of the whites.   On the
occasion of a revival, the only relation of the blacks to it
is that they shovel sawdust on the ground inside the tent.
The pictures of the black church in College Grove, Tennessee, in You Have Seen Their Faces are symptomatic of
Caldwell's life-long sociological approach, urged on and
accompanied by his father, who went with him to see how
others practiced their religion.   At the same time he tries
to show that, as one of the characters in Miss Mama Aimée
says, the black people have their own religion, he also
demonstrates, in quoting the preacher who tells his congregation that God listens to those who give, that the bases
are the same.   In Search of Bisco notes that some blacks
are not black enough to be Muslims.

        The dual standards of the law were/are extremely
important to white dominance of blacks: thus literacy is
crucial to getting either protection from or the full benefit of
the law.   Sam Brinson, who wanders rather heedlessly
through Trouble in July, is portrayed as never really com-
prehending the law.   He is referred to as a fool about cars,
as Geechees evidently often were, not to mention many
whites.   He is constantly trading, is ignorant of the law,
and keeps getting entangled with it.   Unlike the other blacks
who might be found in the jail, he has not robbed a chicken
roost, passed counterfeit coins, jumped bail, or shot up a
Saturday night fish-fry social for the fun of it.   He has re-
sold a mortgaged second-hand car.   In an effort to get him
to be more restrained and realistic in his dealings, he has
been held in jail for a few days but is due to be released
with warning of court action if there are any more mortgaged cars sold.   As this story shows, when Sam is hustled
away by the lynchers as a surrogate for Sonny Clark on the
loose, an unfortunate tendency can lead to the very brink of
death (and doubtless beyond).   The heart of Sam's trouble
is that, probably unconsciously, he does not accept the

white man's law as a reality. His luck holds. Sonny Clark
is, like him, disoriented to the whites' codes; he has no
luck at all.

     Various blacks, like Lee in The Last Night of Sum-
mer, the bouncer in the road house, lived on the edge of
the law, presumably because respectable jobs were hard to
get. He makes marijuana-seasoned burgers and gets liquor
for the house customers. In The Weather Shelter, a black
who wanted to marry an attractive mulatto--to use her as
a prostitute--kills her when she balks. In Tobacco Road,
the black firemen on freight trains throw off coal to their
friends in the cabins. The blacks portrayed in You Have
Seen Their Faces are not at all convinced about the
righteousness of the law. A woman sitting in a cell said
she had only misbehaved. A caption on a picture of four
sets of chain gang leg-irons says whipping and shackling
can not change ideas. A member of a chain gang in another
picture sums up his reaction to crime and punishment by
saying he was born black in a white county. In Search of
Bisco (1965) notes the black attitude that violence and spite
towards whites seems unproductive. In Close to Home (1962)
it is predicted that the psychotic deputy, Clyde, who has
brutally killed a black, will be shot. He is found with
eight bullets in him; suggested again is the theme that the
reactions and attitudes of blacks can be just like those of
anybody else.

V. THE BLENDING OF RACES

Erskine Caldwell's father, the Rev. Ira S. Caldwell, who served as an Associate Reformed Presbyterian minister from 1901 to 1944, thought that blacks and whites could eventually live in peace together. Of integration, he once advised one of his congregation in Wrens, "It will come one day." He was, naturally, aware of the ultimate in integration--sexual intercourse across racial lines, something which had begun, doubtless, in the very earliest days of the races' availability to each other. Not surprisingly, the matter of the blending and mingling of races receives much attention in the works of Erskine Caldwell.

In Search of Bisco records Caldwell's uncle's explanation for why not all blacks have the same color. The various degrees of coloration were caused by the couplings of white men and black women, the men having been plantation-dwellers or soldiers from both sides in the Civil War, and the women, slaves. As stated in Close to Home, it had been going on for a long time but could not openly be acknowledged. In that book, as well as Place Called Estherville, Summertime Island, A House in the Uplands, Journeyman, and The Bastard, there are spokesmen for the idea that a "high-yellow" woman, especially, can give a man special sexual satisfaction. Swayne, of the Place Called Estherville, has never had the experience which he shortly thereafter gains for himself, but he has already observed that, externally, black women are more attractive to him than white women, including the one he is married to. He has heard that at some stage in his life every white man will find a black woman irresistibly fascinating. Not only does he think in terms of physical attractiveness, but he understands that, because all black women know the dire consequences of resistance or negation, they can be approached with greater liberty. Troy, the hard-core bigot in Summertime Island, expresses special desire for yellow females between twelve and fourteen. Since they are more pneumatic

and agreeable than white women, he thinks, they would spoil
anyone from thenceforth enjoying white sex partners. He
has been using black women since puberty. Conversely, he
has an intense and active dislike for black males.

The complexion of Grady Dunbar, the landowner in
A House in the Uplands, suggests black ancestry. It is
explained that Dunbar men prefer mulatto women. After
the passage of months, Lucyanne finds her marriage to
Grady unconsummated sexually. Semon Dye, the rake-
evangelist in Journeyman, says the experience with women
of any race is the same. He notes, however, that black
women are more available and react more deeply. Semon
and his host, Clay Horey, speculate on whether it is better
to stick to one race or the other. The discussion is likened
to considering the merits of one kind of cattle as opposed to
another. Semon says that white girls cry when an affair is
terminated and black girls do not.

The father of Josene, the mulatto who is the main
female figure in Close to Home, is the most prominent
citizen of Palmyra and a candidate for Congress. After a
conversation with Josene, which in a veiled way assures
her that she is right in thinking that he is her father, he
tells himself that he does not regret the experiences of his
youth. He has terminated the relationship, probably of short
duration, which produced Josene. However, Native Hunnicutt, Josene's lover, and a white man, assures his wife
only that she will never catch him "like that"--in the act--
again.

In Close to Home there is also mention of Big Boy
Slot, an abandoned shack area where it had been the custom
of white men and older boys to spend the night with accom-
modating black girls. In Search of Bisco refers to the fact
that crossing the color line was generally looked on as a
maturity ritual on plantations. The new husband in "Honeymoon" is startled to wake up after the wedding night to find
a white arm next to his. He wonders for a moment how he
happens to be sleeping with a white girl. Grady, in A
House in the Uplands, it will be remembered, has never
slept with his wife. He tells her, when she confronts him
with her frustration, that his father introduced him to the
pleasures of the black quarter, that sex with women of a
mixed breed is a hard habit to overcome, and that white
girls are not as attractive or desirable. When Lucyanne

expresses her shock at her husband's intimacy with his
quadroon mistress, he says it is like having a stable of
horses or any other hobby. He considers it stupid for her
to be concerned about the matter. His only reaction when
she reports that she has seen him making love to his
quadroon mistress is to berate her for spying. Similarly,
Native tells his minister that his relationship with Josene
is perfectly natural. Caldwell also provides, in the Native-
Josene matter, the suggestion that, several years earlier,
Josene had made herself available to Native and that he is
the father of her young daughter: perhaps the author put it
in such an indefinite way in order to suggest the hazy,
underground nature of this very thriving interracial traffic.

        Generally the black women, as Kathyanne in Place
Called Estherville, succumb to what they realize is inevitable. Troy says he is constantly looking for black or,
preferably, yellow women. He finds that the best time to
get them is at dusk. He approaches his prey in a vacant
lot, intimidates her, and it seems to work. Zerena, in
The Earnshaw Neighborhood, recalls that white men were
always prowling in Dingy Flat, the black quarter, looking
for girls to have sex with. Some would comply; those
who refused got hit. Zerena tried to hide from that facet
of life, but it was not easy. She finds that her daughter,
Suze, is not afraid of white men. Zerena still has her
doubts, though, and tries to keep her daughter out of the
house where she works, where she feels the man of the
house can usually have his way.

        The employer-employee relationship is one of the
four patterns of sexual association between a white male and
a black female presented by Caldwell. Mention has already
been made of the way the husband of Kathyanne's employer
(and thus theoretically also her employer) successfully mani-
fests his need against her passive and dignified resistance
in Place Called Estherville. As he approaches Kathyanne
with his lusty proposal, a neighbor comes to the door.
Taking in the situation at a glance and understanding a pattern with which he is familiar, he makes a hasty departure.
One can only feel he has been in such a situation himself.
Caldwell leaves his readers with what apparently is the only
possible conclusion, that Kathyanne has given in to what she
feels she can not avoid. He also provides sufficient evidence to allow the reader to realize that she bears his child.
A nuance of the event is that her husband-to-be gives evidence

of his love for her by standing by her through the birth of
the child she did not have means to avoid. It will be recalled that the episode which produced the child caused
Kathyanne to seek employment elsewhere, bringing her substantial economic disadvantage. It is suggested that a dona-
tion of money, arranged through one of Caldwell's decent
doctors, came from the transgressing employer.

The episode of the owner and the quadroon in the
black quarter is central to A House in the Uplands. Sallie
John is aggressive, attractive, and ambitious. She calls
herself to the man's attention, boldly touching him when she
serves at the table; she even has the temerity to sit on his
bed. She feels her combination of physical characteristics
from the two races makes her more attractive to both of
them. She boasts about her affairs with white men; she
says she takes from both races.

Caldwell characterizes the decadent landowners as
generally incapable of reproduction, but does note that the
males are often attracted to black women and that the number of mulattoes and quadroons is increasing. When Lucyanne tells her mother-in-law about her husband's relationship with Sallie John, the elder woman describes the relationship of her husband and his father with black women.
On her honeymoon she heard her father-in-law in a room
across the hall in satyric rout with several black girls.
Lucyanne tells her husband that she could never agree to
sharing him with a black woman, but he says she will have
to get used to it. Additionally, in Journeyman, when
Semon Dye sees that Clay Horey has a high-yellow cook,
he assumes Clay is sexually interested in her and tells him
he has a nice wife, too. Even though it is known that
Grady's father spent time in the quarter as his son is
doing, blacks like Uncle Jeff expect that trouble will come
from the open way Grady is going about his affair.

Grady's father had introduced him to sex through a
visit to the quarter on their plantation. Chism Crockett,
in This Very Earth, does the same thing for his son, Jarvis,
in a different way. Chism takes his uninitiated son along
on an expedition in which two black girls are accosted and
taken to an empty boxcar at the railyards. The story
clearly shows the whites' utter disregard of the feelings of
the girls, who are definitely not interested but who do not
feel there is any escape. The actual event of copulation is

not recorded.   The reader knows what Chism is going to do.
There is no indication that Jarvis participated in any other
way than being as astonished spectator.   The implication is
that he has been given some rather basic attitudes toward
sex and race.   Of course, when black girls involved in
such situations in Caldwell's stories do not see that they
must acquiesce, they are raped.   It is hard to tell the difference between participation based on fear supported by a
biased legal establishment and that which involves actual
physical struggle.   In The Weather Shelter the raping of
attractive mixed-color women by whites is taken for granted
and is referred to with some casualness, the same as might
be applied to hunting rabbits.

        One episode involves an actual rape.   Troy Pickett,
of Summertime Island, has tried to bring sexual satisfaction
to the daughter of the white owner of the skiff which had
been rented to go to the island.   She had escaped him.   On
the way home, he sees black women working in a field.
He stops the truck, and intrudes on the group in his bully-
ing way.   Thrusting aside the objections of the women, including the victim's mother, he takes one of the girls into
the bushes and rapes her.   The white man who organized
the trip and is sitting in the truck is afraid to interfere.
He knows that he will have to put up with some sort of
revenge if he does.   Troy swaggers in telling of his exploit.
He can now consider his trip worthwhile.   He does not forget to slur Duke's mixed lineage.   He taunts Duke about the
manner in which he addresses Duke "properly," strikes him,
and tries to question him about the relationship he accurately
suspects took place in the camp, a relationship he was hoping
to have himself.   When the white organizer of the trip interferes, reminding him of how he lost the other fight,
he promises revenge.   In Troy's demeanor it is possible
to perceive a personality with a sense of inferiority finding
satisfaction in forcing itself into a position of ultimate
physical domination over a representative of the hated-
feared race.

        In Journeyman, Semon Dye manages to get Sugar
into his room, by force of personality rather than through
actual physical force.   When her husband enters the room
where Sugar and Semon are on the bed, Semon points a
pistol at him, calls him nigger and coon, tells him he knows
how to handle yellows, orders him to stay back or be shot.
The husband is shot and falls.   Sugar then takes her husband

away to the woods, where he recuperates. The extent of
Semon's success in fulfilling his desires is left to the
reader's speculation. It would appear he reached only the
preliminary stages. Clay Horey, Semon's host, comments
that although he does not mind blacks' being killed, it is
planting time, and the loss of the man might cause him to
have to do some of the work himself. Semon points out
that Clay has not cared properly for him. He also notes
that the interference of the husband, evidently not expected
(though provided for by the presence of the pistol), was
caused by the fact that he was yellow, rather than black,
and that such people thought they were the equals of whites.
Clay replies that Semon ought to have known the woman
would prefer a person of yellow color, as he considers to
be the custom.

Another area of quasi-rape is the jail. References
in The Bastard, in which the sheriff contracts syphilis from
an inmate of his lockup, and in Trouble in July indicate that
sexual abuse may be expected when a black woman is jailed.
Clyde in Close to Home wanted to jail Josene so that he
could have her sexually. The sheriff in Trouble in July
evidently expects his deputies will put girls in cells so that
they can enjoy intercourse with them. He thinks they should
at least stick to white girls, but he wants it stopped in the
jail altogether. He warns his deputies he does not want to
see the cells full of black girls when he returns from the
fishing trip that an impending lynching is forcing him to take.
Caldwell slyly has the sheriff decide to lock himself in a
cell so as to avoid the pressures of the lynching situation.
He is found, to his embarrassment, the next morning to be
sharing the quarters with a black girl. His wife is deeply
angered and hard to convince; it was ineptitude rather than
lust which caused him to be there.

Caldwell does not neglect the idea that real love can
happen between a white man and a black woman. One of
his early, unpublished poems, consisting of ten stanzas, is
the song of a wandering outcast who stumbles in exhaustion
into a drainage ditch. He finds his head is lying on the
breast of a dying brown girl. Though her mortal wounds
have been received at the hands of a white, she gives herself to him. The ecstacy they found in each other could
not find approval on earth. Another episode, in "Tracing
Life with a Finger," written about 1930, deals with a wounded
man who is tended for a week on the top floor of a warehouse

by a black woman. He goes away and returns two years
later but can not find her. In two cases, Caldwell places
an interracial relationship in competition with marriage.
"Return to Lavinia" is the story of the return of Phil Glenn
to his mixed-blood sweetheart after his marriage. Native
Hunnicutt marries a well-to-do, middle-aged widow while
he carries on a love affair with a younger and very attractive mulatto in Close to Home. He does not make love
to his new wife but rather goes to a rendezvous with Josene,
his sweetheart, where they are interrupted in their love-
making by his frustrated wife.

      Native Hunnicutt is a middle-aged bachelor, the town
fix-it man, who has always just bumped along in the same
community in the same old way. It is hard to understand
why Josene wants him. But she does. When their affair
is brought out into the open, Josene offers to go anywhere
Native wants to so that they can be together. He has already deeply hurt her by marrying, presumably for the
loutish reason that the woman was a good cook. Then he
says he has always stayed "close to home" and always will,
thus precluding the only way their relationship could continue. He has not thought his marriage was particularly
important to their relationship, but it is important to her.
She does not confront him with the fact, but Native is all
take and no give. The book makes the conclusion inevitable
that she has borne his child. However, she is not represented as mentioning it to him, and he evidently does not
know it. His selfish marriage to the widow makes Josene
realize she can have no future with him so she regretfully
withdraws to put her life together on a sound basis. Native
does make some moves to help her, arranging for her to
get legal assistance from the person they both think is her
father, Dalton Burrows, a leading citizen. This is a relationship based on general attraction, mostly physical on
Native's part, and entered into and willingly maintained with
satisfaction to both parties for a year. Josene would have
made sacrifices to continue it; Native would not. Though
he did save her from arrest by the psychopath, Clyde, it
is her absence from the house which causes her fiancé,
Henry Brown, to be murdered by the deputy. Josene's sense
of devotion and dignity, her desire, at twenty-five, to build
a stable and valuable life for herself and her child make her
appear more admirable than Native. Though the relationship
between Native and Josene is outside the law, the reader can
only realize that Josene is a person of dignity and morality.

Native is not without feeling but tends to be materialistic
and selfish.

The most convincing display of interracial love is
given by Grover and Kathlee in The Weather Shelter. They
meet by accident in a storm shelter on Grover's pony farm.
Their physical attraction is intense and is soon consummated.
Grover had not believed that he could cross the color line
in love, but he knows that he loves the woman deeply and
that his feelings are returned. He wants to marry her, but
his lawyer compassionately convinces him that it would not
be possible in that society. He can manage to have her as
his mistress but not otherwise. They want each other sufficiently that they make the best of that kind of relationship.
Out of their love, a son, Jeff, is born. Soon after, she
is shot by a black man who wanted to marry her and use
her in prostitution. Though the boy is raised through adolescence by blacks, the father keeps track of him. Eventually the son comes to know his father and the love which
he continues to feel.

What Grover's lawyer says about Grover's idea of
marrying Kathlee, who is a teacher, doubtless reflected the
reaction of society in general in the South concerning interracial marriages. It would be illegal, even if he could get
a marriage license, which he could not. Even if the courts
did eliminats barriers to such a marriage, the nightriders
would run Grover out, forcing him to give up his pony farm.
The lawyer believes that Grover really loves the woman and
suggests what he refers to as the traditional way--keeping
her without any legal action. He even suggests that Grover
buy her a car so that it will be convenient for Kathlee to
drive out to the farm to be with Grover. He asks him to
postpone the marriage a year and then see. Before that
time elapses, Kathlee has been murdered. Incidentally,
the white women he subsequently marries turns out to be
a lesbian and never does give him any sexual satisfaction.

The suggestion in Caldwell's work is that sexual com-
binations of white men and black women are rather common;
everybody seems to know about them. There is a very effective conspiracy of silence as the relationships cannot
have legal status--interracial sexual union was banned by
laws. Pairings between white women and black men, however, he evidently considered far rarer and much more explosive. A trumped-up relationship of that kind triggered

the lynching in Trouble in July. Though the white men insist that no white woman would give herself to a black man
willingly, the lawyer in Close to Home is convinced that
white women usually take the initiative in such affairs. A
man like Troy Pickett hates all male blacks, perhaps because he senses that they are sexual competitors for black
women. Troy even says, when pressuring one white girl,
that he wants to save her from violation by a black--by
Duke in fact, whom ironically she was indeed trying to
attract. In "Tracing Life with a Finger, " an earnest conversation between two white men is reported: one of them
says it is acceptable for a white man to lie with a black
woman, but he is totally opposed to union between a white
woman and a black man. The sheriff in Trouble in July
says that some whites in rural areas are not particular
about color. He thinks any black has the right to guard
against such dangerous approaches. (In this book the confrontation kills both the girl and the black she falsely
accused.)

     Caldwell remarks (In Search of Bisco) that the danger
of a white woman's being raped by a black is overblown.
If they really wanted to do it, the blacks have plenty of
opportunity; but surely most know of the great risk that a
willing woman will change her story. (The one-sided legal
system makes that sort of claim possible.) In God's Little
Acre the remark is made about how distasteful it is to see
a white woman take a black lover. The occasion for the
remark is Darling Jill's giving herself to the albino, which,
according to the speaker, is just as bad. In Tobacco Road,
it is thought that the blacks have looked Ellie May over
rather carefully, noting both her beauty and her deformity.
Jester thinks the blacks would waste no time in "getting"
Ellie May, if she were left alone. Troy assumes all black
men want to rape white women so they can boast about it.
He gives their potential for sexual encroachment as a reason
for suppressing blacks. A discussion in The Weather Shelter
of whether white men want black women brings forth a mur-
derously passionate response.

     Nonetheless, Caldwell knows that such relationships
do exist and gives a variety of examples in his works.
Ganus, a delivery boy in Place Called Estherville, is determinedly overcome by a young customer who is sexually
hungry and maneuvers him into a position from which he
does not have the will to extricate himself. He finds himself

in a mood where he has forgotten his color. He could not
escape her wishes, because he knew the storekeeper would
not accept his accurate observation that the woman insisted
on taking him to bed. That would be the sort of thing no
black would be able to say. By the same token his sister
could not have filed charges against her white employer when
he used her. As was true for Kathyanne, Ganus loses his
job when the love-making makes him late in returning to the
store. He is, naturally, not able to give an explanation of
what has happened.

          Perhaps the teasing tyranny of the nineteen-year-old
daughter of the house where Ganus had worked played a role
in his succumbing to the widow. Miss Stephena uses Ganus,
who will do anything he can for her, with merciless disregard for his safety. It is her custom to tease him, at times
when she is in her bedroom. Once she challenged him to a
wrestling match for a pillow she was holding in her arms.
He is constantly begging not to have such provocations presented. In the last of their scenes together, she orders
him to get her breakfast, countermanding the directions her
mother had given before she left the house with the girl's
father, leaving the house strategically empty. (The torture
of the contradictions by two all-powerful authorities is like
that in Georgia Boy.) She brings her pajama-clad body
close to his and makes a point of his being aware of her and
the trouble she can force him into. She insists on his thinking what would happen if they were both the same color.
When he asks her to stop talking about his being attracted to
her sexually, she sharply reprimands him for talking back.
Then she commands him to stand on his head. Though he
has not done the stunt for some time, he complies. At last,
he becomes dizzy, and slowly resumes a standing position.
Stephena gives him a hard slap in the face so he will remember to ask permission to stop the next time she orders
him to do something.

          As he stands, hurt and helpless, she orders him to
take her breakfast to her room. As he proceeds to her
room with her food, he has thoughts of how much he likes
being with her and how much easier it will be to get into
trouble in her bedroom. He carefully avoids stepping on
her pajamas, which she has removed upon getting into bed.
When he nervously tries to withdraw, she detains him, just
as her mother had. She is holding a pillow across her
breasts. As she partly exposes her breasts, sitting up in

bed, she demands to know what he would do if he were certain he would go undetected. She gets out of bed, insisting against his protests that he answer, rejecting the pajamas he pleads for her to put on. He reminds her that being observed with her naked would be the worst thing that could happen to him. He tells her he wants to live. She replies by saying she will scream if he fails to do as he wishes. He pleads for mercy. When she promises never to tell, he replies that he wants to believe her.

Standing naked before him, she bites his wrist. As he asks her to stop, she bites deeper. He lunges, trying to escape the bite, and falls, with Stephena on top of him. He instinctively puts his other arm around her neck and holds lightly. Then her body relaxes immediately, and soon she stops biting. She tells him she wanted to know how it would feel to have his arm around her, that she knew she could make him put it there, and that he should leave immediately. As he hurriedly exits, he sees that she is hysterical. She declares in sobbing triumph that he has done her will.

In a very different way, a woman makes a black teenager do her will in The Weather Shelter. The shelter--which had seen the inception of the love affair between his father (the pony farm owner) and the teacher, Kathlee--is where Jeff, a teenager, now finds himself trapped by the bulky, determined wife of one of the neighboring poor white farmers. The scene in which the woman arouses the boy and takes advantage of his reaction, quelling any effort on his part to get away from her lying on top of him, is the most explicit account of intercourse in all of Caldwell's work. Aside from her evident natural lust, the woman has been motivated to rape the boy by her longing for a baby. The reader is left to conclude that the woman's husband gives her neither sexual satisfaction nor the child she wants. Like Kathyanne, who does the will of her white employer, she conceives after the one occurrence. When she delivers the baby, which can be seen to be of mixed blood, her husband draws the correct conclusion that Jeff is the father. An attempt is made to lynch the boy, but Grover manages in an eerie night flight to get him away from the community. The white woman is here presented as just as ruthless in her use of the boy as any white man could be.

In another demonstration of the aggressiveness of white women, Bonnie, a promiscuous woman, is traveling

with two men who come to camp on the same island as the
principal characters in Summertime Island. Duke, the teacher, like Ganus and Jeff, knows she wants him and that she
represents reckless danger. If she is found with him, he
will be the one to suffer. She approaches Duke and a white
boy when they are in swimming. Duke effects their departure from her suggestive and harmful presence. But that
night she makes her way into his tent and involves him in
such a strenuous embrace that his camp cot breaks with a
crash. That eliminates Bonnie from the scene. Happily,
Troy, who hoped he could develop an association with Bonnie, is out on the prowl. Then he comes back and notices
the cot, which the others burned, is missing. From then
on, he suspects that Bonnie has been with Duke. Bonnie,
it should be noted, confides in Duke that she knows he is an
Indian. The lust that broke down the color lines must do
it under a cloak of pretense.

Dene, the wife of Clay Horey in Journeyman, is more
forthright. She tells Semon Dye, the evangelist, that she
has prevailed on Hardy, one of the black workers on their
farm, to entertain her sexually. When she first let him
know her intentions, she recounts, he was so reluctant that
she had to lock him in her room. She told him he must do
what she wanted. After she overcame his reluctance, he
became the most satisfying sex partner she had ever had.
Semon informs her that white women thinking black men are
better than white men is a serious problem. The law against
sexual mixing of races, he recognizes, is not enforced.
He dourly predicts that every one will be yellow in time. It
will be recalled that, in Poor Fool, the black fighter, Knockout Harris, had a white mistress. It is noted that he has to
pay more than usual to keep her, because he is black.

As Caldwell records patterns of interracial sex, he
depicts also both positive and negative reactions to it. Un-
dergirding all of the negative reactions is the fact that miscegenation had long been illegal. That fact, however, stays
beneath the surface. When Native's wife, in Close to Home,
tries to file charges when she discovers her husband and
the black girl, Josene, together, she finds her lawyer quite
firm on the inadvisability of the action and law enforcement
officers very elusive. The situation even promotes a conspiracy of inattention between town and county officials.
Conversely, The Earnshaw Neighborhood's Zerena will not
let her daughter model in a club because it is not integrated.

The promoter, who had no objection to letting down barriers, is informed that any mixing of races not _forced_ _by_ _law_ would cause trouble.

Native's pastor tells him his affair with Josene was sinful. In Journeyman, one of the sins mentioned at a revival is white men copulating with black girls behind the barn. Semon Dye is outwardly aghast when Dene says she has prevailed upon Hardy to make love to her. Caldwell provides an ironic juxtaposition of factors when he puts a fundamentalist preacher in the would-be lynch mob in The Weather Shelter. He leads the vicious group in prayer and declares that it is their duty to track down anyone who has committed the worst of sins, sexual race-mixing.

Race-mixing was officially considered worse than adultery, of course, and thus just that much more of a cause for divorce. Though Native's wife blames Josene for enticing her husband, she wants both of them punished. And, of course, there are many examples of the relationship between lynching and sexual transgression involving both races. In A House in the Uplands, Grady's wife takes it as an especially cruel blow that he goes to a black woman. Mere adultery would not have mattered so much. The shock of discovering her husband with a quadroon woman makes Lucyanne hysterical. She runs desperately out into the fields, rushing aimlessly through briars and into a plowed field, staying out all night. The idea that Bisco's wife (In Search of Bisco) was not light-skinned but rather white was given as a reason for his having to move out of Georgia. The whites thought he was just saying she was a light-skinned black so he could get away with living with a white woman.

Maebelle of Close to Home thinks (wrongly) that no "good" people cross the sexual color line. Zerena, who generally is struggling to eliminate racial barriers, says people of her color want to stay black and avoid further race-mixing. Grover's wife, who is a lesbian, says the worst thing she can think of when she learns of the son born to him and Kathlee--she calls Grover a "nigger frigger." The wife of the sheriff in Trouble in July makes it aggressively clear that she would feel deeply humiliated if she found he had anything to do with a black woman. In the same book, the wife of Sam, the hostage, says black women do not like their men to have anything to do with yellows either.

Two of Caldwell's stories reflect the tension in the

mind of a white wife with regard to the husband's being in
love with a black woman. "Yellow Girl" deals with the
problem of the yellow woman, the wife in the story saying
she would rather have a poor black cook than a good yellow one. She seems to be aware of the attitude many men
have about the extreme desirability of a woman of mixed
breed. The only thing wrong with a yellow woman, of course,
is that she is partly black. The story relates in an under-
stated way the fear the woman has of the yellow cook. Her
inferiority complex makes her feel physically weak and emotionally apprehensive. There is much figurative use of the
relationship between white and brown eggs.

Disappearance of the husband's photograph raises a
question in his wife's mind about the character of a new
brown maid in "The Picture." When she goes to the home
of the maid and finds her husband's picture there, she also
realizes that the brown woman is extremely attractive. The
woman's shock at the discovery causes her to faint but later
she does not mention her trepidation to her husband. The
story ends inconclusively with the wife in the arms of her
husband, but also the maid has been retained, and her subtle
personal attributes, such as the laughter that is different
from a white woman's, represent an unlimited threat.

Naturally, the white men who have children by black
women produce children who tend to have obvious physical
resemblances. A white woman in Close to Home says it is
embarrassing to live in a small town and see constant family
reminders of undoubted race-mixing. She would prefer to
live in a large city for that reason. On the other hand, in
the same book, a lawyer thinks of at least one black child
he has fathered. He is now a twenty-year-old who works
in a sawmill. Looking back on the relationship, he thinks
of it rather pleasantly, as one might steal fruit from a
farmer, something one could not do in maturity. When he
met his son, who did not know his father, he always spoke
to him and was sorry he did not know his name, though he
thought he was better off not to know.

Having a skin color that constitutes evidence of racial
interbreeding is generally represented as a great liability.
Grover, in The Weather Shelter, when an attempt is made
to lynch his son, Jeff, takes him to the town where he
understands Kathlee's mother lives. He has the idea that
the boy can stay with them in the black quarter. But the

boy does not want to stay there. While his grandmother
could have taken the boy, his step-grandfather is very much
opposed and other arrangements are made. Lawana Neleigh,
in Jenny by Nature, says she is part Indian but is taken for
a mulatto. When she looks for a job, she has no offers
but is repeatedly approached on a sexual basis and is nearly
raped. The white men she encounters have no interest in
her except as someone they can exploit, especially sexually.
When her landlady is told to evict her so as to make her go
to the black quarter, the landlady refuses to do this. Thus
the political boss has her home burned down; Lawana, who
had been given a sedative to help her stand all her rejections,
dies in the fire. Caldwell uses the experience of Lawana to
make it clear that he sees the twin bases of racial segregation and racial discrimination to be economic greed and
physical lust. He had been aware of the special problems of
people of mixed racial parentage since he wrote a passage
in "Hours Before Eternity" to the effect that mulattoes do
not laugh as much as blacks.

       However, crossing the color barriers does have ad-
vantages. Caldwell writes that a mythical town has 2300
whites, 1200 blacks (who live in the black quarter), 500
others who have skin light enough they can live wherever
they choose. They can "pass." The lawyer in Close to
Home says that the evidence of race-amelioration is all
around. Many prominent families have both dark and light
branches. He mentions that one of the ways black blood
has been injected into white families was for a black servant to raise a child of mixed blood with the offspring of
the plantation family for whom she worked. The light-skinned
child at some point has to decide whether it is better to
"pass" or not. In Search of Bisco has a note to the effect
that light-skinned people want the black blood to get along
with the white blood. They have a special reason for helping to build bridges rather than barriers. Deep South has
the comments of an Episcopalian, whose mother was white
and his father black: he feels that his mixed blood gives
him insight into both races and that the situation has given
him increased self-confidence.

       The idea that women of mixed race give special sex-
ual satisfaction is mentioned repeatedly. That is the reason
a man of mature years might enter into or continue an interracial alliance. But there is another, rather cold-blooded
reason mentioned. A prolonged affair can be pursued with

no danger of being dragged into a marriage. A white girl
can exert pressures which would necessitate matrimony,
but the law has no remedy for the woman from the black
section. The only disadvantage to an affair with a black
woman, according to many Caldwell characters, would be
that it might spoil the enjoyment of intercourse with a white
woman (e.g., Close to Home).

As Native put it in responding to his minister's
scolding, having a woman of color is as natural as keeping
hounds. The fact that many men thought as he did has
made the enforcement of miscegenation legislation largely a
dead issue. Maebelle's lawyer tells her everyone would
think it a joke if she preferred charges regarding race-
mixing. Perhaps action would be taken in a case involving
a white woman and a black man. The sheriff, in patiently
discussing the matter with her, says he can not interfere
with customary activity so near the election. A complaint
about blacks' not abiding by segregation rules would naturally
be honored. But she wants both Native and Josene charged
and jailed. The sheriff blunts her ardor by mentioning that
he did not think her late first husband would approve of her
charging a black person and a white with the same crime.
That would suggest racial equality.

Just as the lawyer in Close to Home had said that
the evidence of interracial sexuality is all about in the great
range of skin colors and various biological characteristics,
so the doctor who delivers Kathyanne's baby, given her by
rape, calls the quadroon infant very nearly perfect and ob-
serves that people will have to ignore skin color and that
changes will have to come.

VI. PROTEST AND CALDWELL'S ART

As he created his fictions based on life in Georgia
and elsewhere, Erskine Caldwell had in Georgia one whose
heart was in tune with the protest he was making about the
condition of society. On March 17, 1935, Ira S. Caldwell
has published in the Augusta Chronicle a letter which enun-
ciates better than Erskine Caldwell ever wanted to the driving
force of his creative efforts. The elder Caldwell, aroused
by criticism that God's Little Acre and Tobacco Road were
not related to actuality and having joined his son in challenging the newspapers to send their own reporters to see
what Ira S. Caldwell had been working with for several
decades in Georgia and elsewhere, identified his reaction to
the life he had seen. He warned that the people of this
country had been "kidding ourselves" and that "the deadly
cancer of social injustice was spreading in all levels of
our social order. "

He aimed his remarks at a "disease of crushing
poverty" which could no longer be concealed. He expressed
satisfaction that the Chronicle had sent out reporters and
published a series of findings, which constituted "a glimpse
of conditions in Jefferson and adjoining counties. " It was
a beginning, but the condition was spread far wider than
his reportorial coverage, he pointed out.

Some, he said, would say that the poor were the
cause of their own problems. He said thoughtful people
would realize that "every individual is, to a large extent,
the product of his environment, of the institutions that men
have set up, of the social forces that society lets loose. No
man is self-made and no man is self-unmade. " He noted
that people are often exploited by members of the same
church they belong to. He expressed the hope that a new
policy of using newspapers to allow people to be aware of
the danger "in which our social order stands" was about to
begin. He stated his belief that the public would support

newspapers which "will stand like a stone wall for social
justice to all people." Every city in the country needed a
newspaper which had "the courage to make a determined
fight for social justice." Whether the newspapers of the
country occupied a position of leadership "depends on the
attitude of the editorial page towards the social injustice
that is sweeping the vitals of our social order." Ira S.
Caldwell did not mention racial problems per se in that
article, but he knew, as Erskine Caldwell knew, that racial
problems were basically economic; poverty, the identified
target of Ira S. Caldwell's concern, was almost inevitably
attached to blackness.

It seems that Erskine Caldwell, though he certainly
agreed with his father's beliefs and joined him in wanting
to bring social problems to the attention of the public, felt
that his father's methods were not sufficiently subtle to work
in the largely apathetic society which, when it reads, usually
does not do so to learn more about society's problems. He
has consistently disclaimed the role of reformer, though he
consistently wrote like one. Occasionally he does admit that
he has a social purpose; but more often Caldwell has referred to himself as a student of sociology and economics,
believing (erroneously it seems in retrospect) that in college
he pursued those subjects especially. Being the individualist
he will always be, what he perhaps has meant is that he has
had an avid interest in social patterns and the economic
causes behind them. But he generally leaves it to the reader
to sense the serious purpose behind the interesting story he
hopes will attract the reader to the general environment they
reflect.

Probably one of the most undeniable attributes of Erskine Caldwell is his poker face. In a way, he is giving
his contemporaries, whether the people he encounters personally or the readers of his works, an intelligence test.
When he wrote for the New Masses about killings of blacks
in 1934 he specifically said he thought his investigation had
put him in physical danger. He said, too, that he took certain precautions not to be spotted by local law enforcement
officers when doing his observations for In Search of Bisco.
But, more characteristically, he says in Around About
America that he does not worry about receiving personal injury, having once, in New Hampshire, failed to rise when
Kate Smith sang "God Bless America."

The statement he has found he wants to make is that

he is a writer of imaginary tales. The stories must be
interesting enough to hold the reader's interest, for the
writer's purpose fails if there is no reader. The story
must, however, be "profound enough" to leave an impact on
the mind of the reader. He strives to create imaginary
people who will seem more vivid and memorable than real
ones. This is one of the ways in which he uses hyperbole.
When he attracts the reader to the images he has created,
he does not want to be involved in the issue of whether or
not the reader agrees or disagrees with his judgment of
society. In fact, he attempts the rather difficult, and at
times unachieved, feat of criticizing society without necessarily making people aware of what he was trying to do.
Perhaps the most outstanding example is <u>Tobacco Road,</u>
which has been seen by millions of playgoers in an adapted
and weakened version, mainly presented and received as a
robust comedy. The same is true of the book, which has
sold many millions of copies and has helped to create his
reputation as a writer of "sexy" books.

He is perfectly aware that the sexual extravagance of
that book, which represents a kind of personal conduct unlike his own and which he deplores, makes it more interesting, especially for those who otherwise would not receive or
assess the social criticism that is the real motivating force
of the book. The writer saw that sex as presented in Caldwell's works is essentially destructive and frustrating, almost never related to satisfaction in life. Thus he asked
Caldwell if he were attempting to portray sex as tyrannical.
His disclaiming reply was that, "You deal with the inside of
the characters; I deal with the outside." It is this kind of
personal protectivism that causes his friend, Dan Rowan, the
actor, to call him a "put on" artist.

In the final analysis, it would seem that Caldwell has
not trusted society enough to make himself in any way vul-
nerable through revealing his sincere intent to comment on
its shortcomings in the hope of its improvement. He has
found it desirable to keep officially aloof from reactions of
any kind. He is very adamant about not discussing a book
he is writing; he dislikes critics, particularly those of the
academic breed, who seem to him far more interested in
the niceties of remote literary considerations than the serious problems of society. He likes to write a book in accord
with whatever appeals to him, for the most part spending
perhaps eight or ten months on it, and then have the rest
of the time to loaf and/or explore the world, what has been

his consuming passion for approximately six decades.

Perhaps unlike his father, he has no enthusiastic il-
lusions about creating major and immediate social changes,
as much as he might desire them. When Tobacco Road and
God's Little Acre broke upon the American public in the
early thirties, it was evident to some that they were significant social criticisms as well as intrinsically interesting
literary creations. Those who were devoting themselves
to social change could see that he cared about it, too.
Thus, by the early forties, and especially during his marriage (1939-1942) to Margaret Bourke-White, who was even
more enthusiastically liberal than he was, he lent his name
(but never his person, saving his energies always for his
writing) to a sufficient number of organizations to cause him
to be listed in Elizabeth Dilling's irresponsible Red Network.
After he came back from coverage of the German invasion
of Russia in 1941, he felt it necessary to disappoint left-
wing Hollywood writers by telling them, "I am not a Communist and never have been." He is, of course, far too independent a spirit to follow any kind of dictatorship. However, in the McCarthy days, there was enough of an aspect
of social criticism attributed to the name of Erskine Caldwell to make his agent suspect, though proof could never be
found, that he had been black-listed in order that his material would not be used on television. The result seems
to have been that while he maintained his interest and sym-
pathies and published Around About America, Deep South,
and In Search of Bisco in the decade of the 1960's, he had
become independent of organizational relationships, and thus
he remains. He continued to care about the character and
texture of American society, as he had done from the beginning, but he eliminated anything that could interfere with
his independence of action and reaction.

When he applied for a Guggenheim Scholarship in
1931, he gave as his aim to write about what needed to be
done to keep the rest of the population from the economic
level on which the blacks were living. He was in the early
stages of his Cyclorama of the South, which included Tobacco
Road, God's Little Acre, Journeyman, Trouble in July,
Tragic Ground, A House in the Uplands, The Sure Hand of
God, This Very Earth, Place Called Estherville, and Episode
in Palmetto. The reader will recognize that the portrait of
black life as seen in Caldwell's works derives mainly from
these books--Trouble in July, A House in the Uplands, and
Place Called Estherville especially--but, as he was to state

in Around About America, he related the struggle of the
blacks in America to all other struggles for personal, social
and economic freedom. It is typical of him that when in
1969 the United States sent astronauts to the moon, he was
thinking of visits Americans might make to "Skid Row" (or
"Skid Road") and that "certainly none who have been there
want to go back again. " He thought people who knew of the
still-existing poverty areas would wonder why such places
still existed while reading about or watching the moon trip.

    Though the extent to which Caldwell's consciousness
of America includes concern about interracial problems has
already been explored, a few other aspects relating to his
hopes and dreams may be noted. In Around About America
he wrote that he thought the joining of races should depend
on the personal choices of the individuals involved. He
meant that their desires should not be stemmed by society.
He thought racial blending could bring about a kinship that
could eliminate racial warfare. He thought then (1963) that
the black campaign for equal treatment would continue and
that its successful culmination by 1970 was likely. In
Search of Bisco contains the comment that enforcement of
social and economic racial mixing would result in destruction
and violence. It would appear that the situation which he
portrays in The Weather Shelter (1969) holds the most hope
for him. Grover Danford fell in love with a woman of mixed
blood, Kathlee Bazemore. They could not marry in the legal
and social climate in which they lived. They consummated
their love and produced a child. The mother was killed by
a black who wanted to exploit her. Later, Grover discusses
with his teenage son, Jeff, the difference between the sexual
union which created him and the acts which produced the
white strains which can be seen in so many people with
dark skins, wherever they live in the country. Grover tells
Jeff that he existed because his parents loved each other and
wanted him because of their love. He admits that he does
not know how long it will be, possibly decades, before
unions such as that one can be considered normal.

    Though The Earnshaw Neighborhood (1971) was con-
cerned largely with a portrait of a white woman, Caldwell,
as the reader will recall, uses Zerena White to express the
views of an independent, middle-aged black woman and her
even-more-independent teenage daughter. He also uses more
than a page for a discussion of the label used on the jars of
Frank Earnshaw's Goober Butter. It shows two small boys,
barefoot, one white and one black, dipping peanut butter out

of the same jar. A white grocery store owner comments
that he does not think Martin Luther King could have thought
of a better symbol of potential racial harmony. The peanut
butter tastes the same to people of all races, and observation of this fact is used as the occasion for pointing out that
races can live together successfully if bygone prejudices are
not taught. Caldwell seems to have chosen his rather ordinary white speaker to suggest that the ideas he is present-
ing have occurred to many people in Georgia, the locale of
The Earnshaw Neighborhood, and doubtless elsewhere.

On being questioned in May 1973 about progress in
solving racial problems, Caldwell said he found the situation about as he had recorded it in his writings. "The only
thing is that some blacks are getting affluent. What that
will do, I don't know." He felt the question is what effect
better housing and more goods will have. "The more affluent they get, the more they will want to move into white
neighborhoods." The thing to watch will be what happens
when the blacks have money enough to move into the suburbs,
he thought. He did not think he saw any important change
in attitudes of either blacks or whites. The next day he
gave the commencement address at Erskine College, in Due
West, S.C., and included the solving of racial problems as
one of the battery of difficulties which needed the graduates'
talent and attention.

Erskine Caldwell has been trying to see humanity as
it was, as it is, and wrote of it for the sake of what he
hoped it would become. Scientific progress, he has felt,
must be accompanied by reaching a state of general respect
for the individual person. The goal of society, for Erskine
Caldwell, should be to produce good citizens who can live
anywhere.

Addendum 1. THE GEORGIA CRACKER*

My first impression of the importance of Georgia was received when I entered one of Atlanta's numerous second-rate movies, and was greeted by the following slide: "Lest We Forget--We Live in Atlanta, Georgia, the greatest city in the greatest state in the world." And the press, also, consistently spreads the news that Georgia is a state flowing with wild honey and its people the cream of the earth. For instance, I quote this editorial by Harlee Bramch, one of Georgia's leading figures, which has appeared in the Christian Science Monitor, the Atlanta Journal, and numerous others newspapers and periodicals:

> No state in the Union has produced a longer list of distinguished men and women than has Georgia, which has supplied the country some of its greatest statesmen, most distinguished soldiers, most eloquent orators and most noted educators, historians, poets, writers, authors, musicians and business men.
>
> No state in the Union has a purer strain of Anglo-Saxon blood running through the veins of its people.
>
> No state is troubled less with the problems of foreign emigration [sic].
>
> No state possesses a finer culture or one more typical of the old south.

This booster spirit has taken hold of everybody in the Georgia Commonwealth. Rotary and Kiwanis are not the only organizations, as you see, in the field--in all parts of the State, at every cross-road, there is something or someone waving the banner of boosters and windbags. However,

---

*By Erskine Caldwell. First published in the November 1926 issue of the Haldeman-Julius Monthly; reproduced here by permission of the publisher.

I was a newspaper reporter during my stay in Georgia, and
so in spite of what the citizens think--or would like others
to think--the truth about the Georgia Cracker filtered through
to me.

Education and enlightenment in the Cracker state are
of small importance to those living there. The highest pin-
nacle of success being that of politics, which notoriously
has no mental prerequisites in that part of the South, there
is naturally no reason why money should be wasted on high
schools and universities--money is sorely needed to adver-
tise Georgia, you know. A grammar school education in
the state is proper and legitimate; a high school education in
centers of large population is passed over without comment
by the natives; but to enter a college is to be looked upon
with suspicion. It is generally thought that a high school
education is ample for teachers and professors--and so it
is, for the most part.

And Georgia has taken to Literature, too. Not in
Atlanta alone are the followers to be found, but in all the
one-horse country villages. Each community now has its
Literary Club and reigning local authority on the subject.
The Literary Division of the Woman's Club in one of Atlanta's
suburbs reported for December 5, 1925, the following:

> In her original manner, Mrs. W. E. Whitehead
> gave a short sketch of Jean [sic] Stratton Porter,
> telling just enough of her delightful book, The
> Keeper of the Bees, to create a desire to see the
> presentation of this story of nature and romance
> now appearing on the screen at one of the local
> theatres.

Georgia keeps and honors Corra Harris, while Frances New-
man has had to seek new fields. When William Lyon Phelps
visited Augusta during the winter season, due mention was
given him as the "greatest living authority on literature," in
the Augusta Press.

Although I have placed it second in this discussion,
religion ranks foremost in the hearts and minds of the
Crackers. Baptists, to be sure, lead all the rest numer-
ically, but the Methodists and Presbyterians follow closely.
Nor do these three denominations have the field to themselves. With the possible exception of Alabama and Mississippi, Georgia suckles more Holy Rollers, Snake Charmers,

and the like, than any other state in the Union.

I recently attended a camp meeting where the preaching had been in progress for three weeks. The congregation was in the act of speaking the "unknown tongue." Everyone was keeping time with the music by swaying from side to side and jerking his head. In the midst of this a young girl suddenly appeared on the scene. She jumped from her seat and tore her outer clothing from her body. The congregation seemed to find nothing unusual about the procedure, and the head-jerking continued. The girl began dancing up and down the aisles mumbling unintelligible words, pulling her hair down about her shoulders and kicking her shoes off her feet. There she was, clothed only in a scanty piece of underwear, using her stomach and hips to great advantage, but the bowed worshippers took no notice of her actions. The exhibition continued for more than fifteen minutes, during which she sported herself like a hoochy-coochy teaser, a contortionist, and epileptic recovering from a fit. At last she ran out of the church into the arms of one of the male preachers, who quickly carried her off into the darkness.

At another evangelistic gathering in the woods of Georgia I was introduced to the "Snake Charmers." The snake was strongly guarded in a crackerbox. When the minister was ready for this act on the program he called for the reptile to be brought out, and amid much flourish and excitement a young woman, it is always a young woman, grasped the squirming snake around the neck, a very advantageous position. Thus holding the choking reptile with a viselike grip, she flourished the dangling body around in the air. When the poor snake was all but dead, the entertainer then brought its head in contact with her powdered breasts. The serpent, being too weak to answer back, merely hung his head. I am told that whenever, in these "Snake Charming" performances, the young woman is unable to go through with it, the preacher charges her with insufficient faith. I have never seen a preacher with faith enough to perform the act himself.

A number of years ago, when I was in my 'teens, I visited in Georgia. At that time there was a Holy Roller meeting near where I was staying, and one evening with several other boys I went to view the spectacle. While the rolling was in progress we threw a handful of flat-headed tacks through a window on to the path of the onrush. Three of us were caught in the act and carried bodily into the midst

of the exponents of physical culture, where one of the clergy-
men told us to get down on the floor and roll our sins away.
A buxom woman weighing not less than three hundred pounds
was there on the floor beside us, and since she was apparently unable to make a complete revolution, I gave her a
hand. Once started, she could not stop, and rolled with
gaining velocity down the aisle in the direction of the two
preachers, whose backs were turned. If the three had been
football candidates, they could not have done better--the
two apostles shot backward simultaneously, their heads
cracking the uncarpeted floor. Those two men of God were
familiar with more oaths than any laymen I ever heard, but
possibly that was because they knew more of the words.

There has been so much agitation about the treatment
of prisoners in Georgia, that in 1925 the State Legislature
appointed a special committee to investigate. Crucifixion of
unruly convicts by stretching their arms against a fence and
fastening their wrists with ropes drawn through holes in the
fence, then standing them on a narrow two-by-four and passing
a steel rod behind their legs in such a position that the
knees are drawn forward and the prisoner hangs by his heels
and wrists, is too brutal a method of punishment for me to
administer, declared Warden R. H. Roberts of the Ware
County Convict Camp. Warden Roberts showed members of
the committee such a contrivance in his camp, installed, he
said, in accordance with suggestions given him by the State
Prison Commission. In Wayne County extremely bad cases
were handcuffed over a crossbeam, with their toes just reaching the ground. This is a report of the conditions found by
the committee in one place, and yet nothing has been done to
remedy them.

A short time ago Milledgeville was the scene of one
of the most disgusting cases of mob violence in the history
of the state. A Negro--it was a Negro, of course--was a
patient at the State Sanatorium for the Insane, suffering from
violent insanity. In a sudden seizure of the disease, in its
most dangerous stage, he killed his white nurse. The citizens of the town did not consider that he was not responsible
for his actions, or he would not have been in an insane
asylum, and the news dispatched told this story:

> Willie Dixon, Negro, who last Tuesday attacked
> and killed Miss Amy Oxford, nurse at the asylum
> at Milledgeville, with a pick handle, was quietly
> carried from Colony Farm two miles from the

asylum, into Wilkinson County by a small band
of men.   He was chained to a tree and beaten to
death with a pick handle.   The body of the Negro,
still chained to the tree, was found early today.
The pick handle used as the instrument to produce
death was found nearby.

Nothing was done by the State in this case; nor will
any steps ever be taken in the case.   And indeed, the number of citizens who are ashamed of the fact that their brothers will lash a demented person's head with a pick handle
is so small as to be negligible.

But in spite of Georgia's barbarism in education, religion, and justice, we still might believe its boast that "no
state possesses a finer culture or one more typical of the
old south. "   So let us look to the oldest and wealthiest family
in the state, the Chandlers of Coca-Cola.   During the opera
season of 1926, when the Metropolitan Company, of New
York, spent a week in Atlanta, this family occupied nightly
two of the most prominent boxes in the house.   During inter-
missions boys carrying trays went about the audience.   Well,
the ladies in the Chandler party spread their handkerchief
over their laps, the gentlemen spread their handkerchiefs
over their stiff-bosomed shirts, and they all drank Coca-
Cola straight from the bottle.   The ladies did use a straw,
I believe.

So this is Georgia--whose inhabitants do cruel and
uncivilized things; whose land is overrun with bogus reli-
gionists, boosters, and demagogues; whose politics are in
the hands of Klan-spirited Baptists; and yet whose largest
city boasts of being the "greatest city in the greatest state
in the world. "

Addendum 2. HAPPY BIRTHDAY, DEAR ERSKINE!
... and many happy returns, Georgia Cracker!*

I hope this secondary salute from a Southern friend, on your anniversary, will not disturb you--or Georgia. I do not send it, as some other, more sensitive old neighbors down this way might, as the crack of a wagoneer's bull whip on a tobacco road. It is dispatched as an overdue endearment from one who, like you, loves the hard, swept earth under the chinaberry trees and not merely the perfumed miasmas beneath the magnolias. And I send it with special enthusiasms this year. I put them, like candles, on your cake:

First and least: In the year just past, the number of the buyers of your books passed forty million. That's a lot of books. Hard-backed and paper-covered, they amount to more than all the volumes in The Library of Congress, which has more books than any other library in the land. In using that comparison, I am not proposing a national library composed largely of paperbacks--though few of the great books ever written would be left out of one that was. Actually, it seems to me more important that so many books are in the hands of people and not merely on the shelves of an institution.

Second candle: You are not only the read, but the young and the damned, too. Perhaps I should have been as impatient last summer as I am sure you were with the folks about Augusta, Georgia, who like to think of the South as a place in which Eisenhower plays golf. They showed themselves glum with you, still, when you wanted to film God's Little Acre there. Maybe their hospitality in providing authentic local scenes and characters for the story of Ty Ty

*By Jonathan Daniels. First published in the December 1957 issue of Town and Country, pp. 115 and 117. Reprinted here by permission of the publisher.

Walden and Darling Jill was not all that you, old boy from
down the road in Wrens, had a right to expect. Their hostility to the project was pretty good evidence that stories you
wrote a quarter of a century ago give still-erect Georgians
the jerks such as an evangelist like your Semon Dye might
only have hoped to produce at an August meeting. You may
be damned in Georgia, Brother Caldwell, but you sho' ain't
dead. And neither is the film millions will be waiting to
see.

Third and brightest candle: You have confounded
those who thought that they were able to condescend about
your books. Some of them, of course, never understood
you. They thought, as some Georgians did, that you were
helping them look down their noses at Georgia, not realizing
that you were never writing about Georgia but always about
man. The worst were those critics who were shocked to
discover that your work--which first appeared to their se-
lect delight in such avant-garde publications as the Double
Dealer of New Orleans and old Gene Jolas' transition in
Paris--was being read by people who purchased their reading matter in drugstores and bus stations. The smart world
which praised you from a telephone booth found, fastidiously,
that your universal appeal left them in the Grand Central
Station at 5:15. If they're going to catch the train, however,
they'd better look, as at the clock, at William Faulkner's
recent listing of you (naturally, along with himself) among
the five top contemporary American novelists. This is rare
praise, indeed.

All year round, and not merely on a birthday, it is
easy to see that there is nothing new about either the Georgians with the civic jerks or the jejune critics.

We've had time for a man's maturity since Congress-
man Braswell Drue Deen, of Georgia, rose in the Congress,
in 1936, to demand that the cops close Tobacco Road. Con-
gressman Deen came from Alma, Bacon County, where then
one in ten people couldn't read you or anybody else. Well
over half of its people were tenants. Mr. Deen had been too
small in size for the Army in World War I, but had grown
to the presidency of a junior college in Gene Talmadge's
town of McRae. He did mighty battle against your stories
of Georgia people. But he ended his oration with a real
complaint which has steadily confounded both Georgians and
critics since. "You cannot buy tickets, " he said sadly. "It's
all sold out. "

Perhaps more significant, there was Alexander Woollcott. He was more important to you in the days when you seemed to be about to break the record for literary-garret occupancy set by Oliver Goldsmith. Woollcott then was the petted power among critics. He made his speech through a crack in his door to which he had invited you for a drink and then forgotten it. "Go away," he said. And you told him to his face that, even in a rich, figured, red-brocade robe, he looked "like a fleshy, elderly woman in a Mother Hubbard."

Woollcott could take it. Your realism pleased him. You got the drink. Not as happily or as quickly, perhaps, others may open the door--even advancing Georgians who come to recognize you as a devoted prod and not a damned plague--even the critically fastidious who have regarded it as impertinent that millions seek the work which the daring discovered. Appreciation moves to your door by the millions. Only you, Erskine, I think, will not change. Even in sending my birthday wishes, I have a feeling that birthdays are irrelevant festivals with you.

At fifty-four, a man born at White Oak, in Coweta County, Georgia, ought to have cracks a quarter of an inch deep in the back of his red neck. Or a rivet in it. Instead, you look everywhere like a quiet, gentle, thoughtful, sharp-eyed traveler who naturally loves the purple shadows on the mountains about Tucson and the white mists which climb the hills at San Francisco. But I decline to be misled by your mature appearance, even on your birthday. The inescapable truth is that you are still--and millions intuitively understand that--the colt-legged Georgia boy who grew up in the sand-clay cotton country in East Georgia.

Your biggest birthday blessing is that as a writer you are still the tow-headed, wide-eyed boy by the rutted road staring at the wagoneers and the drivers of Tin Lizzies, too; at the restless women, the bent old people, and weary young ones; at the head-long and the left-behind; the hungry and the lecherous and the lightheaded. You see for us as a boy might see, with fascination and without fear--though not without pity--the realities that hunger is not the only greed left to the poor, that humor is not the prerogative of only the rich, and that God in Georgia and elsewhere moves not only in a mysterious way but also often in an amazing company.

You have let us see the wide, yet often cramped,
world with the morally and socially unencumbered eyes of
the boy on that road that ran by your house, not only
through the pellagrous passages of Georgia, but also to the
cold woods of Maine and the strange places beyond Smolensk.
Maturity can be the development of the mind or the accumu-
lation of deceptions. What girls on buses and old men on
trains realize unconsciously, as they read you, is that no
one in our times has a less clouded retina of remembrance.
You have kept Huck Finn's eyes in a life which is always a road as well as a river. God knows, you are not
Peter Pan, who constituted a boyhood imprisoned forever in
the ideas elders expect always to preoccupy the young. They
will classify you, by-and-by, as a realist, humorist, folk-
lorist, even sociologist. On your fifty-fourth [i. e., 55th]
birthday, I myself would cast you as one of the eternal
children in Hans Christian Andersen's The Emperor's New
Clothes--and rejoice in the joint consternation of some
Georgia patriots and literary snobs. The Georgians are the
less naked of the two.

Indeed, it wouldn't surprise me, Erskine, if Georgians
one day erected a monument to you, like the one they have
in Augusta now to the Georgia poets nobody in Georgia any
longer reads. Then Georgians would emulate Enterprise,
Alabama, where, in a blooming economy escaped from cotton, the people raised a memorial to the boll weevil which
had relentlessly taught them the way to better living. I
have less hope for the literary snobs who distrust any art
which appeals to many besides themselves. But they make
less difference. There will be no monuments for them anywhere. Their proper place is in criticism's potter's field.
Certainly not at anybody's birthday party, yours least of all.

[Note on early Caldwell publications: The Double Dealer,
which is quite accurately referred to by Mr. Daniels as of the
kind of publication which published Erskine Caldwell's first
stories, never in fact printed any of his work. His first
published story, "July," appeared in transition in June 1929.
In October 1929, the third volume of an anthology of work
of young writers, The New American Caravan, was published;
in it was "Midsummer Passion," the same story as "July"
except that language changes had been made. Being certain
that transition had forgotten it or lost it, Caldwell submitted
it a second time. Other small literary magazines which
published Caldwell stories early were Blues, Pagany, and

Hound & Horn.   His first book, The Bastard, was published
at the end of 1929.   The June 1930 issue of Scribner's included "A Very Late Spring" and "Mating of Marjorie."]

Addendum 3. ERSKINE'S LITTLE ACRE*

Yesterday's audacity is today's routine. Creative
work that once seemed outrageous may set future standards.
Thomas Wolfe was the scandal of Asheville, N. C. Today,
his relics there are a major tourist attraction. Several
decades have much altered public opinion concerning Manet's
Déjeuner sur l'herbe, and Paul Chabas's September Morn.
Audiences once seriously debated the propriety of Tannhäuser
and La Traviata--household operas by current judgments.
And though certain readers, including no few Georgians,
were disturbed by Erskine Caldwell's earthy early novels--
Tobacco Road (1932), God's Little Acre (1933), etc. --these
works are now regarded as modern classics.

Generally, however, Caldwell's first novels were
warmly received. First reviews saluted an important new
talent. But his fellow Georgians were more deliberate about
bestowing their approval. Their reluctance may seem odd
today, when college classes everywhere study the implications and aesthetics of his writing, and when Georgia ad-
mirers are among those who propose him as the worthiest
American candidate for a Nobel Prize in literature. But
among early Georgia readers of Tobacco Road and God's
Little Acre, there were many who deplored his subjects.
"Let sleeping dogs lie, " they advised. They were less concerned with enjoying fine, new books than with protecting
their state's good name, and they wondered if Caldwell's
subject-matter--regardless of accuracy--appertained to just
that aspect of Georgia life they liked to see publicized.

However, Tobacco Road was not only a hit novel, it
soon became a stage play that was to run for seven years

*By Frank Daniel. First published in the September 1968
issue of Atlanta; pp. 78, 79, 84; copyright 1968 by Atlanta
magazine; reprinted by permission. Bracketed material
supplied by Frank Daniel.

on Broadway, and road show performances were announced
for Atlanta. Local anti-Caldwellians organized and sprang
into action. The now defunct Board of Film Review, a
klavern of opposition, got its authority extended to include
stage plays, and set about trying to suppress performances
of the play in Atlanta. The effort failed, however. Earlier
in this decade, a comic-opera legislative committee weighed
the wisdom of suppressing God's Little Acre, which, by then,
had sold more than ten million copies the world over. It
gets harder all the time to start even the most modest
lynching-bee in Georgia.

William B. Hartsfield, Atlanta's mayor in the 1940's
and 1950's, liked to boast that Atlanta had never suppressed
a book, and the current mayor, Ivan Allen, Jr., could say
the same. But during the 1930's, it may be recalled, many
Georgians diligently explained that Tobacco Road wasn't
"typical"--as if King Lear, for instance, is of consequence
because Lear and his daughters were a "typical" royal
family.

A Caldwell contemporary in Atlanta recalled his own
reaction upon reading the Caldwell books: "I felt caught
red-handed," he says. "It was as if Jeeter Lester and Ty
Ty Walden were my responsibilities. And such guilt must
have increased as the early Depression years showed how unprepared we were to help the needy and alleviate their
troubles and their suffering. I tried telling myself that
Caldwell's broad, bucolic humor was reminiscent of Huckle-
berry Finn and typically American. But I laughed guiltily.
Levity seemed out of place though it intensified the violence,
tragedy, and underlying sociological insights in the books.

"I have an idea such stories, so real, so immediate,
had a strong influence on the welfare legislation of recent
decades. Caldwell lifted his characters from their 'pockets
of poverty' and planted them at our front doors, in our consciousness and on our consciences. If, today, Caldwell is
no longer 'shocking' he is still powerful, and his realism
now seems fervent and forthright to anyone familiar with
the casual candor of more recent novelists."

The Victorian Era lingered in Georgia until World
War I. By the time Tobacco Road was published, the sub-
sequent Jazz Age had come and gone, but many of the Georgians who first pronounced judgment on the novel were products of the century's turn--hardly exponents of a dance

called the Charleston or habitués of the speakeasies. Locally
indeed, the 1920's were never quite as gay and carefree as
today they are represented as having been. The state was
largely agricultural, and that was the decade that brought the
boll weevil to our cotton fields, often already depleted by
soil erosion and decades of tenant farming.

        Georgians were as given to reading thirty-six years
ago as they are today. They enjoyed the output of Faulkner, Hemingway, Wolfe, and Caldwell as up-and-coming
novelists--not as the landmarks they have become. Georgia
then had a fair crop of writers, some of them as dedicated
as Flannery O'Connor's freak prophets. But in the Depression decade, Caldwell's realism struck readers as unique.
From the first, Caldwell wrote about deprived and suppressed
people, about the inarticulate and unrepresented, and a writer
of his sort in the South during the 1930's would inevitably
deal with the racial attitudes in an era when the topic was
considered of minor interest as far as the general reader
was concerned. A contemporaneous specialist in Negro
stories, Roark Bradford, certainly produced wonderful
stories, but they are remembered for their charm, quaint-
ness, and entertainment value rather than for any darker
qualities. A New York publisher, to whom Georgia writer
Lillian Smith submitted Strange Fruit in the early 1940's,
rejected it because of its racial theme. As he explained
it, relations between white and black people were a subject
of highly specialized and negligible interest. Yet Caldwell
scenes in which Negroes are involved are among his most
vivid and vigorous, and their impact remains today. Has
any writer dealt more effectively with interracial feeling
than Caldwell in Kneel to the Rising Sun, published in 1935?

        Caldwell's early life prepared him well to deal with
the oppressed and poverty-stricken characters in his books.
He was born in a nameless community near Moreland,
Georgia, in Coweta County. His father was an ordained
minister, secretary of home missions of the Associate Reformed Presbyterian Church. The family moved about once
a year, sometimes more, living among rural members of
their denomination throughout the South. The young Caldwell
spent most of his first twenty years in Southern "pockets of
poverty." He went to Erskine College (his father's alma
mater) in South Carolina, the University of Virginia, and
the University of Pennsylvania; and, as he pointed out recently, graduated from none of them. "I took nothing but
courses in economics and sociology," he related. "I couldn't

be bothered to take other courses required for a degree."
Economics and sociology were highly pertinent subjects in
the 1930's--the years that brought Caldwell's first fame.

By coincidence, Caldwell and Margaret Mitchell
worked simultaneously on the Atlanta Journal in the mid-
1920's. Both were aiming, even then, to write--in the
current phrase of the times--the great American novel. By
coincidence, they both did. They realized their ambition
because they were great storytellers, but they each also had
a bit of luck on their side. The 1920's saw the appearance
of no generally read Civil War novel. By the time Miss
Mitchell published Gone With the Wind (1936), war was a
vital thought in people's minds. Nations were arming for
World War II, and GWTW anticipated it in familiar terms
of the past. In the same way, the characters and conditions
Caldwell deals with most effectively commanded the attention
of a vast audience during the Depression years--just the
time Tobacco Road arrived on the scene.

"My interest in writing about the South," Caldwell
says now, "came into being because one, I had a desire to
write, and because two, I knew no other life to write about.
I had no interest in what other writers had written. I
was interested in only what I could see and hear."

Caldwell is a purely professional writer. He starts
work at nine or ten o'clock each morning, and works until
five in the afternoon--seven days a week. He is, in fact,
a born writer, and any other occupation is a means to an
end, and the end is a story. His autobiographical Call It
Experience (1951) is concerned with how he came to produce
salable manuscripts and with his seven-year apprenticeship--
after which he has nothing further to say in the book. In
a volume called Writing in America, Caldwell foreswore
identification with any cult of literature. "As the word has
become defined in my own mind," he said, "literature implies
a graceful treading along a prescribed course and a slavish
conformity to the sensibilities of prejudiced minds. For that
reason alone, I have no desire to belong to that community
and be obligated to abide by its rules and regulations, because I am not quiet-spoken...."

Caldwell's approach to writing ruled out any influence
by other writers. "Everything and everybody provided the
germ of a story," he says. "Having the good fortune to be
living in those years from Virginia to Florida to Tennessee

was more than an abundance--it was a heaping bounty of
things and people.   The idea for a story [or novel] may have
started in one locality and been transported to a series of
localities.   But always these were Southern things and
Southern people and the feelings and implications I got were
changed from one locality to another.   A novel about a
school teacher might have been written about South Carolina,
but it could just as well have been Alabama.   Nevertheless,
Georgia was always the focal point, perhaps because I knew
it and its people the best of all. "

There was, said Caldwell, "no conscious cataloging.
Stories came one after the other with no plan other than to
hurry and write about this and that.   And they came so fast
that I had to eliminate a lot of good ones.   For instance,
there were those people in that house over there, there was
that [white] man keeping a colored mistress, there was the
eleven-year-old girl pregnant and getting cussed out by the
preacher in church, and so on and on.

"I was a simple novice in writing, and still am, and
I had to write only about that which could be seen and felt
and heard.   Every hour or two was a story in itself.
Trouble was, I couldn't write the stories fast enough, because I was a novice, and wanted to get them so right that
I wrote them time and time and time again to be satisfied.
I didn't read much.   I was too busy living and trying to
learn how to write a story.   Why read when you want to
write something for other people to read?   And today I don't
read any more than I have to.   I'd rather try to write
something myself. "

Caldwell denies that he literally turns fact into fiction, that his fictional characters are reproductions of real
people.   "There's nothing mysterious about the Tobacco Road
characters, " he says.   "I never knew anybody who became
a character in the book.   But I knew hundreds of people
who might have become characters.   You put them all together.   You let them put the story together.   Then after-
wards, you can single out dozens and dozens of people who
might have been real in life.   You can't put real life into
fiction--you have to make fiction real.   This is why fiction
is more real than life. "

Early this year [1968] Caldwell and his wife were in
Atlanta where he spoke at DeKalb College.   Mrs. Caldwell
was interested when, after the lecture, a member of the

audience said to her that her husband had been "before his
time, " writing of racial tensions and adjustments in the
1930's--"a generation ahead. "

"My interest in writing about Negro life, " Mr. Caldwell says, "and its relation to white life, probably derived
from my high school years in East Georgia.   This was the
agricultural area where both black and white were in misery
of some kind.   The white sharecropper of the Tobacco Road
era was one kind of economic and social misery.   But the
Negro of the time was far worse off.   No use saying why--
everybody knows why.   I think I came to know the Negro
because I happened to live in a town [Wrens] where a chain
gang [all Negro] was quartered for a summer while doing
road work.   During those months I hung around the gang
camp on Sundays [instead of going to church] and got to know
many of the Negroes from fifteen years of age upward.

"Sunday was the day off for the chain gang and the
people on it could get out of their cages [many with ball
and chain] for several hours and shine shoes for a nickel.
Somebody would come along selling bags of goobers for a
nickel, and you could sit there and share the peanuts and get
a shoe shine while the boy or man told you everything about
his life.   He may have got on the gang for spitting on the
white man's sidewalk, or not paying [because he couldn't]
a five-dollar fine for something or other, or stealing peaches
from his landlord, or dozens of other reasons.   Anyway,
this was where a person could talk endlessly about himself
and anything else and you could hear about a lifetime of
economic and social misery. "

Of his boyhood, Caldwell says: "I grew up in the
Great Depression in Georgia.   I know how poverty smells
and feels.   I was poor as to eating.   Poor as to clothes.
Poor as to housing.   And nearly everybody else was too,
and you can't know about poverty any better way.   You
don't like it and nobody else does but you can't help yourself.   So you learn to live with it, and understand it and
can appreciate how others feel about it. "

At sixty-five, Caldwell writes assiduously, daily,
devoutly, as compulsively as some men play golf.   It's a
lifelong habit.   Hence, it's no surprise to note that the
newest edition of Books in Print lists fifty Caldwell titles.
A fifty-first--Deep South--appeared earlier this year.   It
is non-fiction, subtitled Memories and Observations, and it

discusses the religion of Southerners, as he observed it in
youth, and as he has seen in recent years.   August sees
the publication of a new novel, Summertime Island.   (Its
scene is Mississippi, near Memphis.)   Still, Caldwell says,
he writes very slowly, and he rewrites several times before he is satisfied.   It takes about a year for him to produce a book.   Georgia Boy took three years, the longest
time he has spent on any one book.   Caldwell readers circle
the globe.   His books have been translated into dozens of
languages.   He is not a book-shelf author.   He is read pro-
digiously, and estimates that about seventy million copies of
his books have been sold.   God's Little Acre leads.   Tobacco
Road has sold over five million along with its success on the
stage and screen.

Caldwell's Tobacco Road and John Steinbeck's The
Grapes of Wrath (1939) are probably the most poignant accounts of life during the Depression years.   Yet it has been
pointed out that, when Tobacco Road appeared in 1932, Caldwell had been living out of Georgia for several years.   How,
then could he write so vividly of Georgia?   The answer is
that Georgia, as already mentioned, suffered a local depression, especially severe in its cotton-growing areas, during
the 1920s.   There is no year specified in the novel.   But
Georgia had been depressed almost constantly since the Civil
War.   Caldwell had seen many jobless, hopeless, needy
people before the Stock Market crashed in 1929.

The scenes of Tobacco Road are clearly indicated
as taking place in what Caldwell calls "pockets of poverty"
in rural Georgia.   Remembering how passionately early
Georgia readers of the novel insisted that the characters
weren't "typical, " it is interesting to note how painstakingly
Caldwell was to emphasize their exceptional situation.   The
middle-aged woman preacher, Sister Bessie, and her teenage
fiancé, Dude Lester, walked from Jeeter's depleted farm to
the nearest village to buy an automobile and a marriage
license.   When they reached the automobile sales office in
the small town of Fuller, the salesmen are so astonished
at these customers that they can hardly seal the bargain,
and Sister Bessie gets her license to marry Dude only over
vigorous objection at the ordinary's office.   One of Mr.
Caldwell's best and most timely volumes of non-fiction is
In Search of Bisco, published in 1965.   Here again he is
careful to make distinctions.   Its pages also reflect his un-
failing insight and sympathy:

The plight of the uneducated and prejudiced white Southerner, or poor buckra, as he was sarcastically named by the Negro years ago, is a pitiful one. This man of ill will is between forty and sixty years of age, barely literate due to lack of educational advantages in his youth, who is economically handicapped for life because he is now and has always been an unskilled laborer.

One of the common evidences of the poor buckra's frustration is his gullible eagerness and fanatical desire to be duped in inflammatory exhortations of the designing, scheming, rabble-rousing, opportunistic, professional politician.... Having little within himself in which he can take pride, and habitually frustrated by his awareness of his past, present, and future economic and social poverty, the poor buckra resents any achievement of the Negro and retaliates by doing anything within his cunning to restrict and deny the rights of all Negroes....

The urbanized Atlanta Negro, in contrast to the frustrated poor buckra, is the fortunate beneficiary of the most extensive educational complex of any American city. This educational system has been segregated from the beginning not by the Negroes but by the discriminatory customs of the politically dominant white race.

Atlanta's many schools, colleges, and universities for Negroes came into existence as the result of the determined efforts of the Negroes themselves to provide higher education and professional training for Negro teachers, lawyers, and doctors barred from enrollment in the public and private institutions reserved exclusively for the white race in the State of Georgia. This determination to provide higher education for Negroes has made possible the present trained leadership of authentic spokesmen for civil rights in Atlanta, in Georgia, in the South, and throughout the nation.

Despite the length of time Caldwell has been writing of the plight of the Negro, the "poor buckra, " the dispossessed, and the unfortunates in our society, one often gathers the impression that commentators on his newer work

are not always familiar with the over-all body of his work.
They seem sometimes unaware of the powerful social commentary in such novels as Trouble in July, for example, as
well as the earliest of his short stories.   They can give
the impression of assuming, because Caldwell avoids literary
devices and poses, that he is a simple man.   Originality
and vitality, on the other hand, have made him a lasting influence in American writing.   But very likely the absence
of coteries and courtiers have militated against a more general recognition as one of the strongest and most lasting
voices of our time.

Addendum 4. "GOD'S LITTLE ACRE": AN ANALYSIS*

[The editor's note to this article explained that it was intended to be a scientific analysis of the "perplexing phantasies" in this work and others. It was intended to "supply
a basis for a later literary estimate." Readers of Caldwell
will find it stimulating.]

        Men have always known that the romantic picture of
love and marriage is false. They have known that the eager
yearnings of adolescence meet with strangely bitter disap-
pointments in the effort to translate themselves into the realities of adult experience. Only recently, however, has
any understanding come of why this is true, through the
realization that, from childhood on, each step in Everyman's
psychosexual evolution is taken in the face of opposing forces
which threaten to drive him from the path of normal development. If then the impulse to write and to read bears any
relation to human needs, it would seem to be inevitable that
a struggle which begins in earliest years and continues
throughout life must find insistent expression in literature.
It is not strange, therefore, that novelists and readers have
always been concerned with sex.

        To meet the needs of different temperaments, how-
ever, literature assumes varied forms. The simplest and
most childlike response to disappointment is to retreat into
phantasies in which the frustrated yearnings are gratified.
In this way simple people can console themselves with the
adolescent and sentimental prevarications of the movies and
the cheap magazines. Even the better forms of the romantic

---

*By Lawrence S. Kubie, M.D. First published in the No-
vember 24, 1934 issue of Saturday Review of Literature,
pp. 306, 307, 312; copyright 1934 by Saturday Review Co.;
reprinted with permission.

novel serve essentially the same simple need.   Such writings
might therefore be called the romantic and consolatory literature of sex.

More complicated temperaments cannot make use of
this elementary device of phantasy and romance; but instead
react to disappointment with bitterness and irony, which
expresses itself in an effort to belittle that which is unob-
tainable.   Much of the so-called "classical" erotic literature
satisfied the needs of such readers; Rabelais and Casanova,
Boccaccio and Cellini.   But whether it be naive or sophisticated, romantic or ironical and bitter, all of this literature
constitutes merely varying forms of literary escape.   In
neither group is sex recognized as a serious, perplexing,
and vital human problem.

Out of the modern temper, however, there has arisen
a third group of books; one in which sex is treated frankly
and seriously, and yet with a confused pattern of tension
and distortion.   These books form the great bulk of the so-
called morbid modern literature, a literature which attempts
not merely a safe and literary escapade in sex, but rather
a mirror of the moving realities of sexual problems in all
their intricacy.

Certainly a compelling drive to portray and solve the
problems of sexual unrest and dissatisfaction is not an obscene or morbid purpose.   Yet just as the problem play will
be violently attacked while the naked revue passes unmolested,
so, too, the cheap and "sexy" magazine, or the subtler wag-
gery of classical erotica, will be accepted unprotestingly by
the very people who raise the cry that these modern books
are deliberately capitalizing [on] the morbid and perverse in
human nature.   In other words, an honest and vivid literature, which is struggling to express the confused problems
of sex, arouses such hostile, uncomfortable, and suspicious
feelings, that it is attacked as dirty, obscene, sick, useless,
ugly, etc.   This is a strange and paradoxical social phenomenon, the explanation of which may lead to a deeper understanding of the psychological and artistic significance of these
books.

The most obvious point is that the protesting reader
has been made uncomfortable in a special and peculiar way.
Furthermore, not only is he uncomfortable, but he is resent-
fully aroused as well; and it is out of this constellation of
feelings that he throws up the epithet "obscene."   To define

what is meant by obscenity is impossible, because the word
does not carry quite the same implications to any two people.
Nor is there any one type of scene or phrase which will
make all people squirm. Yet the experience is almost universal, a feeling which everyone has encountered and can
recognize, even if its effective stimulus varies from one
human being to another. And since it is universal, it must
have some common underlying quality.

This experience might well be called the "sense of
the obscene," and with regard to it we will take as our
premise: (1) that a reader's phantasies, be they conscious
or unconscious, arise from his personal needs; (2) that this
angry, resentful sense of the obscene arises when confused
and troubling unconscious phantasies are stirred into activity;
(3) that this happens when such phantasies have been
awakened in the reader by the vigor of the author's art.

From what has been said already it should be clear
that our search leads directly into the problem of psychosexual illness. The difficult lifelong struggle towards adult
normality is pursued through a maze of infantile and childish
impulses, which, though normal enough at their own levels,
become disturbing if they persist with dominating force into
adult life. It is inevitable, therefore, that in a literature
which deals with a blind groping towards normal sexuality
one should find much of the psychopathology of sex drama-
tized in literary expression. This will appear chiefly in
descriptions of adult distortions of infantile impulses; and
it is just here that the reader, either for lack of technical
knowledge, or because of inner problems, is most likely
to mistake the portrayal of distorted sexual development for
the manifestations of a supernormal lustiness and release.
Often enough the picture of sickness is taken for an example
of a greater freedom. It becomes therefore a most difficult
problem to estimate the esthetic significance of this confused borderland between sickness and health.

Since no problem in science or in art can be solved
by generalizations alone, our first step must be to subject
a typical example of this literature to a frankly psychoanalytic
scrutiny. To do this one must use the tale and the people
and their words as dreamlike products of imagination, dis-
secting the story for the conscious and unconscious content
of the characters' minds or acts to see how much of sickness or of health lies within its pages.

For this purpose we have chosen the novel, God's Little Acre, by Erskine Caldwell, first published in the spring of 1933 by the Viking Press. It is an earthy and vivid story of Southern whites, who struggle in the land, and in town, and in their bodies to reach some kind of peace. And because here and there this struggle is infused with activity which is technically known as "perverted," the book drew upon itself the curiosity of all and the wrath of many.

In the tale, as in a dream, there are confused and kaleidoscopic shifts forwards and backwards between desolate farm land and a turbulent strike-weary mill town; from deep pit holes in the red and yellow clay to hilly eminences, from swamp land to solid earth. Unlike an actual dream, however, the movement from scene to scene is carried along on a thread of story; whereas in a dream which has not been artificially elaborated the episodes would follow one another without even this pretense of conscious reason. To the analyst, therefore, the story serves as a rationalization, an effort to give an appearance of logical order to the sequence of free phantasies. This conscious elaboration of spontaneous phantasy succeeds in making the tale appear simple and realistic; but it also interjects elements which are extraneous to the fundamental dreamlike structure. It is necessary, therefore, to confine the analytic interpretation to the main outlines of the story, considering only the characters and their outstanding acts.

As in many dreams, one may recognize two groups of characters, those that are clear and those that are vague. There are some shrouded and ominous figures who hover dimly in the background, like those unseen persons in a dream whose presence one senses but never sees. There are others who stand out with all the hallucinatory vividness of the lions and tigers of a child's nightmare. Their clarity is a tribute to the author's skill, particularly because, despite their sharp outlines, they retain their fantastic and unreal quality; and when closely examined these figures fuse until they seem to become different aspects of a single human spirit, split up by a legitimate and effective literary artifice into resemblances of separate beings.

Among all the characters one finds no living mother in the book. Yet everywhere throughout the tale brood the spirits of unhappy, frustrated, and forgotten mothers, dimly seen, yet constituting the essential but unrecognized object

of all the conflict which the story contains.   The figures of
women can be arrayed in order from the most dim to the
clearest; and then one sees that the shadowy figures are the
frank mother-images, and that as the figures of women become clearer the maternal role is distorted more and more
towards perversion and prostitution.   It is as if the book
were saying that the only good woman is a dead and legendary
mother--and that even there danger and sin may lurk.

      First there is old Mrs. Walden, who, before the tale
is begun, has died of heart-break because her oldest son
was ashamed of her.   She is a dim phantasy of a good
mother, dead and therefore forever unattainable.   Then
there is the witch-like figure of Gussie, supposedly diseased
and hoarding gold, whom the oldest son had married and
with whom he hid himself away.   This is the "bad woman,"
the "sterile mother," no mother at all and yet more mother
than wife, who is heard wandering eerily off-stage and who
never appears directly in the action of the book.

      The first woman to emerge even dimly from these
shadows is Rosamond, Ty Ty Walden's oldest daughter, and
the wife of Will Thompson.   She remains vague in outline,
but at least she is alive.   She weeps in the background of
the story, taking humbly and gratefully what Will has left
over to give her, mothering him, feeding him, spanking
him with her hair-brush when she catches him _flagrante
delicato_ with her younger sister, Darling Jill.   Then she
tries in a sudden rage to shoot him; but in the end she
mourns his death in a paroxysm of grief.

      And finally come the only two clear and vivid women
in the tale, standing as the direct objects and instruments
of primitive lusts.   One is Griselda, the wife of Buck
Walden, the daughter-in-law in the Walden family, no mother
in spirit or in fact, but whose body stands to all the men
as a perverse symbol for nursing.   The other is Darling
Jill, the youngest Walden daughter, who devotes her life
to conquering men with her body, insatiable and destructive,
tantalizing men, using them, throwing them aside, demanding
pain as her only physical joy, and turning for peace at the
last to the fat, infantile, and eunuchoid figure of "Pluto."

      This much, then, can be safely concluded: that in
this tale are found only certain limited conceptions of women.
There are good mothers who are dead, good mothers who
suffer, bad mothers who hoard their sustenance and will not

share, mothers who breed and transmit disease, erotic
mothers whose babies exist only to nurse men, and women
who exist only to destroy.   There is no image of a woman
whose body is to be loved as an adult--genitally, confidently,
happily, tenderly, reproductively.   By some undefined magic
of the moon, as Ty Ty Walden says, no act of intercourse in
the book results in the conception of a child.   In the confused and childlike phantasy, babies would seem to be conceived and born in some other manner; and, as we shall see,
sex itself comes to mean either nursing or destruction.

It is the result of a deep inner logic then that the
book is a story in symbolic language of the struggle of a
group of men to win some fantastic kind of sustenance out
of the body of the earth, the "body" of factories, and the
bodies of women; and that the living women struggle through
the mazes of a queer, disjointed, erotic travail to give
sustenance or death to the bodies of men.   Throughout the
book the recurring themes are those of food (watermelons,
hams, grits, and ice cream); or of biting, grabbing, sucking, and licking; and of haunted efforts to rend or tear or
suck or bite out of the bowels of the earth a golden magical
food.   Furthermore, since in the tale nursing and intercourse have become confused and interchangeable yearnings,
it is logical that the chief protagonists should chant obses-
sively the beauty of a woman's breasts, that the woman's
body should always be described in unreal terms more ap-
plicable to a man's, and finally that the woman's body itself
should be transformed into a fantastic well at which a man
may slake his thirst, and ease with his mouth a torment of
neurotic and perverse cravings.

But who are the men in this confused and fantastic
tale, who play out their needs against these figures of
women?   First, there is Ty Ty Walden, an old man and
a widower, seeking endlessly for gold by digging into the
bowels of his farm, rendering his land sterile with mounds
of earth from fruitless excavations.   Despite his years he
digs as a child might, because his "Daddy" told him there
was gold in the ground, and because of the echoing rumor
that negroes have found nuggets.   His gold fever is an obsession, which in his life has taken the place of women and
drink.   He is sensitive, visionary, a mute artist with an
eye for beauty in painting and an ear for beauty in words;
but he lives out his lusts and fears at a childlike level.
With his words he arouses other men's fever equally to hunt
for gold or to assault his daughter-in-law, Griselda.   But

for himself, he is afraid of women, afraid that they "wear
a man to a frazzle. " He is willing to look at them but not
to go too near them; and even when he looks upon Darling
Jill in the very arms of Dave, he does not take in what he
sees, but stands uncomprehending as a child. With his eyes
he feasts on the body of his daughter-in-law, Griselda, yet
he thinks of her and his yearning for her as though she
"were inside" him, as though his erotic impulses were "the
rising up of something deep within" his own body. And he
carries this feminine identification further by likening himself and Griselda "to a hen with a lone chick. "

As an expression of these strange phantasies we find
that his objective energy is directed solely towards tearing
things out of the earth as if it were a human body; and that
when the ground won't yield it up, he flails it like a reluctant living thing. Nor is it strange that he talks of science,
yet resorts to a negro "conjur, " until finally he effects a
confused compromise between the white man's science and
the negro's magic by capturing in a swamp the albino, Dave,
to use him as his divining instrument, an all-white figure
fashioned out of the black mud with which to combine white
magic and black.

Furthermore, to Ty Ty the things of the spirit also
lie within the body. His formulation of religion is that
"God resides inside one, " that "there are secret things hidden in every man, " that "one hunts for the things that are
inside and brings them to the outside. " Thus it is clear
that his gold hunt, his erotic obsession, and his religion
are all part of one confused and largely unconscious system
of obsessive phantasies. He is fascinated and yet terrified
by that which lies within the body. Therefore he cannot
approach the body; and though he is an old man, he is still
a child, interested in the outside that he can see with his
eyes, an aged Peeping Tom. Finally, and like a baby, he
is concerned with the earthy products of the body, prizing
that which other men discard, heaping mud-pies while he
hopes to find in the mud the seed of a supreme and golden
treasure.

Will Thompson is Ty Ty's son-in-law, the husband
of Rosamond. He is the effective instrument of Ty Ty's
frustrated desires; for it is through Will that Ty Ty mates
with both of his daughters and his daughter-in-law. By
trade Will is a weaver of cloth who lives and works in the
town; yet it is his obsessive ritual to tear cloth into tiny

pieces the garments of Griselda when he is about to attack her. For Will, then, intercourse, "to turn on the power," must be preceded by a rending or tearing or deflorating; whereas weaving is like repair and restitution. Will is thus portrayed as a violent man, a "male man" to the negroes, the man whom all women seek and whom all other men hate and envy. With his own words, he likens himself to an almighty and omnipotent phallus. When aroused, his whole body plays this role. He compares his strength to that of "God Almighty." Yet all of this megalomanic phantasy of power can be punctured by a bullet; and in the end he is punished by death for his presumption, that is for his assault upon Griselda and his assault upon the mills.

Thus the bravado and pretended invulnerability of Will cover simple human weakness; and like all weak mortals he must restore himself with food, the most primitive of all restoratives. So Will is pictured as a hungry man who eats as the women wait upon him, and who is brought home by the lure of food; and in his final frenzy it is the mouth which becomes the focus of all his erotic desires. To Will, as to an infant, the most fundamental contact between bodies is through eating; and because his expressed phantasy of himself is of his whole body as a phallus his mouth becomes the instrument of the phantasy.

The other five male figures are less clear and less important fragments. Each of them is dominated by anxiety. None is in any true sense living. These figures of men nurse and dig and beat and threaten, or they peep and yearn and blush. They never love. They never procreate. Their women are either dim shadows of mothers out of the past, or destroying women of the vivid present. It is out of the stuff of phantasies such as these that sickness itself arises.

It is necessary to stress the elimination of the author from our study, because the book has frequently been spoken of as "sick," a characterization which might be taken as meaning that the author was sick as well. Such a deduction is not at all warranted on the basis of what is evident from the book. The relationship of an author to his work is always complex; and to judge of an entire man from an isolated fragment of his stream of conscious or unconscious thought would be both unscientific and unsound. We can speak with some measure of confidence only of that which we have in hand, namely the book itself, and draw no conclusions about the author.

Readers of the book can be observed directly, however, and one finds them to be variously affected. Some
are carried away by the compelling picture of unchecked
passion, finding in this a vicarious freedom from their own
habitual restraints.   Others react with violent and unhesi-
tating aversion.   More often, however, they are likely to
be fascinated, repelled, and puzzled, all at the same time,
hardly knowing whether to envy the characters for their
unchecked and hypothetical lustiness, or to look down upon
them as sick and bad.   Thus we find the reader either caught
by the lure of illness which masquerades as primitive power,
or stirred by deeply buried impulses within himself which
respond to the picture which is painted, or yet revolted at
times and resentful of a note of arrogance which he may feel
in the protagonists of the tale.

It is inevitable that a book which stirs deep and confused phantasies or feelings must exert a fascination upon
the sensitive reader.   Whether in any individual in whom
such confused misconceptions are active, the inner turmoil
will ever break out in active sickness is a matter which
depends upon too many variable factors to allow of any generalizations.   One can say with confidence, however, that
among healthy readers it is unlikely that such a picture of
illness could cause a serious disturbance, and that it is
highly probable that anyone whose precarious balance could
be upset by the book would have been shaken in any case by
the pressure of his own sick inner needs.   One need not
feel too anxious, therefore, about the influence of the book
upon the health of the reader; although one may deplore the
confusion which the book may churn up within him.

And still, perhaps, the question remains, why such
books are, or should be.   To that the only answer possible
is that they are because they have to be.   As long as there
is a group of people who cannot be fooled or consoled by
romance, whether it be cheap and tawdry or delicate and
sophisticated; as long as there are those who refuse to
content themselves with the cold comfort of an ironical
sneer; and as long as those who reject either of these
escapes have courage and honesty, there will be a literature
which seeks to write its way out of confusion and restraint
into some pathway of passionate relief and happiness.   It
would seem to be inevitable that in all such literature the
portrayal of illness must play a role.

For some readers one may be sure that there is

achieved at times a therapeutic relief of feeling through the translation of inner problems into literary forms. For society at large, the question of the value of this literature is more difficult. On the one hand, such books to some extent inevitably break up bigoted and inhibited attitudes towards the body; but on the other hand, when, as in "God's Little Acre," the values are confused, the book may seem to attempt to set up as standards of high normality forms of behavior which are in reality the expression of potential sickness. In all probability, with the passing of years, and with the deepening and clarifying growth of psychoanalytic knowledge, and the subjection of this new material to the needs of art, much of this confusion will gradually be eliminated. In the meantime it must be borne in mind that the search for beauty leads through strange fields; and that to touch deep chords in human nature, even those instinct with illness, may have subtler values than it is possible as yet to characterize.

BOOKS BY CALDWELL ILLUSTRATING RACIAL PROBLEMS

The Bastard. New York: The Heron Press, 1929.

Poor Fool. New York: The Heron Press, 1930.

Tobacco Road. New York: Scribner's, 1932.

God's Little Acre. New York: Viking Press, 1933.

Journeyman. New York: Duell, Sloan and Pearce, 1935.

Kneel to the Rising Sun. New York: Duell, Sloan and
        Pearce, 1935.

Some American People. New York: R. M. McBride and
        Co., 1935.

You Have Seen Their Faces. New York: The Viking Press,
        1937.

Southways. New York: The Viking Press, 1938.

Jackpot. New York: Duell, Sloan and Pearce, 1940.

Say: Is This the U. S. A. ? New York: Duell, Sloan and
        Pearce, 1940.

Trouble in July. New York: Duell, Sloan and Pearce, 1940.

Georgia Boy. New York: Duell, Sloan and Pearce, 1943.

Tragic Ground. New York: Duell, Sloan and Pearce, 1944.

A House in the Uplands. New York: Duell, Sloan and
        Pearce, 1946.

The Sure Hand of God. New York: Duell, Sloan and Pearce,
        1947.

This Very Earth. New York: Duell, Sloan and Pearce,
        1948.

Place Called Estherville. New York: Duell, Sloan and
        Pearce, 1948.

Call It Experience. Boston: Little, Brown and Co., 1952.

Courting of Susie Brown. New York: Duell, Sloan and
          Pearce, 1952.

Gulf Coast Stories. Boston: Little, Brown and Co., 1956.

Jenny by Nature. New York: Farrar, Straus and Cudahy,
          1961.

Close to Home. New York: Farrar, Straus and Cudahy,
          1962.

The Last Night of Summer. New York: Farrar, Straus and
          Company, 1963.

Around About America. New York: Farrar, Straus, 1964.

In Search of Bisco. New York: Farrar, Straus and Giroux,
          1965.

Miss Mama Aimée. New York: The New American Library,
          1967.

Deep South. New York: Weybright and Talley, 1968.

Summertime Island. New York: Weybright and Talley, 1968.

The Weather Shelter. New York: The New American Li-
          brary, 1969.

The Earnshaw Neighborhood. New York: The World Pub-
          lishing Co., 1971.

Annette. New York: New American Library, 1973.

Note: The Pocket Book of Erskine Caldwell Stories (New
York: Pocket Books, Inc. 1947) has the following stories
relating to the racial theme: "The Negro in the Well,"
"Man and Woman," "Martha Jean," "The Medicine Man,"
"Yellow Girl," "The People vs. Abe Lathan, Colored,"
"Big Buck," "The End of Christy Tucker," "Nine Dollars
Worth of Mumble," "Candy-Man Beechum," "Saturday After-
noon," "Kneel to the Rising Sun," "The People's Choice,"
and "Hamrick's Polar Bear."

SELECTED CRITICAL REFERENCES

Beach, Joseph Warren. "Erskine Caldwell: The Comic
Catharsis." In: American Fiction: 1920-1940.
New York: Macmillan, 1941.

Burke, Kenneth. "Caldwell: Maker of Grotesques." In:
The Philosophy of Literary Form. Baton Rouge:
Louisiana State University Press, 1967.

Canby, Henry Seidel. "Introduction" to The Pocket Book of
Erskine Caldwell Stories. New York: Pocket Books,
1947.

Cantwell, Robert. "Introduction" to The Humorous Side of
Erskine Caldwell. New York: Duell, Sloan and
Pearce, 1951.

Collins, Carvel. "Erskine Caldwell at Work." Atlantic
202 (July 1958) 21-27.

_____. "Introduction" to Erskine Caldwell's Men and
Women. Boston: Little, Brown, 1961.

Frohock, W. M. "Erskine Caldwell: Sentimental Gentleman
from Georgia." Southwest Review 31 (1946) 351-59.

Gossett, Louise V. Violence in Recent Southern Fiction.
Durham, N.C.: Duke University Press, 1965.

Hazel, Robert. "Notes on Erskine Caldwell." In: Southern
Renaissance, edited by Louis D. Rubin, Jr., and
Robert D. Jacobs. Baltimore: Johns Hopkins Uni-
versity Press, 1953.

Korges, James. Erskine Caldwell. Minneapolis: University of Minnesota Press, 1969. (University of

Minnesota Pamphlets on American Writers, No. 78.)

McIlwain, Shields. The Southern Poor-White from Lubber-
    land to Tobacco Road. Norman: University of Okla-
    homa Press, 1939.

MacLachlan, John. "Folk and Culture in the Novels of
    Erskine Caldwell." Southern Folklore Quarterly 9
    (January 1945) 93-101.

INDEX